"The Christian way of life does not end when the grace of God grants eternal life to a new believer. Since I was saved in 1962, rarely have I heard any pastor preach or teach on this long overdue subject – the spiritual heart. Steven Ellis, a longtime personal friend, has accomplished what I call a "Bobby Bonds". Bonds was a professional baseball player and a homerun-hitter. Bonds didn't just knock the ball into the stands. He literally hit the ball over the stands and into the ocean. With his book, "A Model for Evaluating Our Spiritual Heart", in a manner similar to Bonds, Ellis has hit the ball into the ocean. Those who give time to read, study, and apply the content of this book will discover their long sought-after post-salvation life that they had heretofore only dreamed."

Dr. James A. Brettell, pastor, teacher, and Christian entrepreneur in ministry to the deaf, Christian school, radio, counseling, and youth and adult training camps.

"Author, Steven J. Ellis, put it best when he said. 'Without vision, we fail and lose hope and belief.' *A Model for Evaluating Our Spiritual Heart* provides a Biblical guide for the reader to look inside him/herself as they search for God's enlightenment in their life. Every reader will want to take their time walking through the pages of this text."

Janie Stubblefield, Professional Counselor

A MODEL FOR EVALUATING OUR SPIRITUAL HEART

Navigating Through a Sea of Notions Toward the Shore of Clarity with a Biblical Model of the Spiritual Heart

Steven J. Ellis

Adonai Roe Publishing

Dallas, Texas

Copyright © 2020 Steven J. Ellis

Published by Adonai Roe Publishing, P.O. Box 671295, Dallas, Texas 75367

All rights reserved. No portion of this book may be reproduced, stored in a retrieval system, or transmitted in any form or by any means – electronic, mechanical, photocopy, recording, scanning, or other – except for brief quotations in critical reviews or articles, without the prior written permission of the publisher.

Unless otherwise noted, Scripture quotations are taken from the *ESV Bible* (Wheaton, Illinois: Crossway, 2008).

ISBN: 978-1-953436-00-9

Contents

Acknowledgements 9

Dedication 11

Chapter Summaries 12

Introduction 15

Chapter 1 – Our Greatest Need: Congruent Hearts Aligned with God's Heart 19

    We Have a Heart Problem 21

    The Word "Heart" Appears 757 Times in 706 Verses 22

    God Has a Spiritual Heart and Humans Have the Imago Dei 23

    This Truth Impacts Lives 24

    The Bible Affirms God's High Valuation of the Spiritual Heart 25

    References to the Spiritual Heart in the Old Testament 27

    References to the Spiritual Heart in the First Century Scriptures 37

    What Do These Observations About the Spiritual Heart Tell Us? 42

    Synonyms for the Heart in Scripture 43

    Toward the Shore of Clarity 44

Chapter 2 – Let's Begin with a Common Language 49

    The Necessity of Defined Terminology and Concepts 49

    A Definition and Description of the Conceptual Components of the Spiritual Heart 50

    Highly Integrated Components 53

    In the Beginning… 54

    The Fall in the Garden – The Consequences of Belief in Distorted Truth (Lies) 55

Chapter 3 – The Vocation of Being Human: We All Have Needs . 60

    We Begin with Needs 61

What are Needs? 66
What are our Beliefs? 69
The Wisdom of the World Leaves Us Thirsty 72
Spiritual Heart Health 74
Chapter 4 – Behaviors: Portals of Insight into Flourishing or Failing 78
   Behaviors of Israel—Portals into the Mixed Beliefs of a Religious Society and Culture 78
   The New Believers of Corinth – The Disadvantage of Beliefs and Behavioral Baggage 80
   What We Believe to be True Is the Basis for Our Behaviors 82
   Anthropocentric Beliefs Lead to Self-Deification and Misplaced Identity 86
   The Path to Spiritual Heart Renewal 88
   Where There is Change, There is Pain 90
   Behavior-Based Portal Examples 93
Chapter 5 – Strongholds: The Fortification of Worst Practices 109
   Strongholds of the Spiritual Heart in Corinth 109
   "Arguments and Every Lofty Opinion Raised Against the Knowledge of God" 113
   The Destruction of Strongholds – How? 114
Chapter 6 – Who We Were, Who We Are, and Who We Can Be 117
   The Dichotomy Within the Spiritual Heart 118
   The Problematic Dichotomy 119
   Pain Accompanies Change 123
   Christ Dwells in the Spiritual Heart Infused with the Truth 129
Chapter 7 – The Best Helper 132
   The Divine Helper 133
   The Divine Helper in Prior Ages 134

The Divine Helper During the Transition Period of the First Century A.D. 136

The Divine Helper Permanently Indwells and Ministers – Content of "Filling" Changes 137

The Importance and Relevance of the Holy Spirit and the Spiritual Heart 139

Clarifying the Understanding of the Helper for Us Today 140

So Today, What Does the Helper Holy Spirit Do? 147

Chapter 8 – When Hearts Align 151

What God Wants Us to Believe for Our Hearts to Align to His Heart 152

Aligning Our Heart to God's Heart: Making Positional Truth an Experiential Reality 153

We Construct the "Old Self" Over Time – Consciously and Unconsciously 154

The Trial and Error Process of "Old Self" Development and Refinement 156

The Good News – Restoration and Renewal of the "New Self" 158

The Process – Putting Off the "Old Self" and Putting On the "New Self" 162

What is Spiritual Maturity Then? 165

What Our Hearts Look Like When Aligned to God's Heart 168

Two Illustrations in Contrast: Saul and David 171

Glossary of Terms 176

Bibliography 178

About The Author 180

Acknowledgements

I want to thank Al Rosenblum ("Al") of Birmingham, Alabama and Dr. James A. Brettell ("Jim") of Little Rock, Arkansas for having provided the seedbed of thought from which this book germinated. The impetus for this book began with a series of virtual online meetings in 2010-2011 hosted and facilitated by Al, Jim, and me. We met online with others from our respective congregations who wished to join via WebEx on Sunday evenings for almost a year.

Al's ministry focus is counseling and biblical studies with particular emphasis upon the spiritual heart. Al has a master's degree in counseling from the University of Alabama, Birmingham. Jim's ministry had been focused over his long pastoral career upon biblical teaching plus practical ministries such as founding and operating a Christian school, church for the deaf, radio, missions, youth camps, and food distribution to the underprivileged and underserved. Jim has invested a significant percentage of his time to studying and teaching in the area of the spiritual walk of the believer in the Lord Jesus Christ. During this period, I was working full-time in my professional career and teaching online Bible studies to a small international audience, the evolutionary stage of what started as a home Bible church in the late 1990's.

All three of us had a similar foundation in the relevant biblical and systematic theological approach to the Holy Spirit and the spiritual (versus carnal) options for living the Christlike life. However, as a result of Al's training and practical work in Christian counseling, the need for greater clarity and applicability of the model we each possessed had become quickly evident. Al had begun to rethink and expand his understanding of the spiritual heart and our online sessions became a means of vetting terminology and concepts as we pursued greater clarity.

I also want to thank those from our respective congregations who joined us online, asked questions, and helped us identify areas needing clarification. This book reflects my personal interpretation and further elaboration upon the subject. There is more to be done. It is not the end, but the beginning.

Dedication

This book and any proceeds generated from it are dedicated to the missionaries and ministries supported by *The Church of the Servant King*. A list of those individuals and ministries can be viewed under the "Ministries and Missionaries" tab at cotsk.org.

Chapter Summaries

Introduction
What a difference would understanding the spiritual heart from a biblical perspective have made forty-five or even twenty-five years ago in my life? How might I have been a more effective, positive, and redemptive influence—a better representative of Jesus, a better friend, a better leader, and teacher?

Chapter 1 – Our Greatest Need: Spiritual Hearts Aligned with God's Heart
Our innermost being—what exactly is that? To most of us, that description of the spiritual heart is more of a notion than something practical, useful, and concrete in meaning. What does the Bible actually say about the spiritual heart? How is the spiritual heart described? If we wish to define and describe the spiritual heart from a biblical perspective, we must first inspect the evidence, the testimony of the key witness, the Bible. The number of references to the spiritual heart will surprise even those who have read their Bible for years. These observations provide the foundation for a definition and description of the spiritual heart – a definition and description that navigates us through the sea of notions and toward the shore of clarity. We discover that our greatest need is for our hearts to align to God's heart.

Chapter 2—Let's Begin with Common Language
Effective communication requires defined terminology. Amorphous or ambiguously defined terms create confusion while we float in the sea of notions. A biblical definition of the spiritual heart promotes fruitful analysis, discussion, and critical thinking. The phrase "spiritual heart" embraces the immaterial and material nature of humans. It is the repository of the *beliefs* and *values* which inform our *expectations*, *emotions*, and observable *behaviors*. It represents the combined function of soul (eternal nature) and body (temporal nature). The fall of the first humans in the Garden was the result of belief in a lie to be the truth. We are all in the same boat seeking clarity—a clarity that only will emerge with clearly defined terms and concepts. In chapter 2, I present a proposed definition and model for the spiritual heart that provides a framework for processing the plethora of information in the marketplace of ideas

concerning our *needs, desires, beliefs,* and *behaviors,* yet many times leaves us asking—"what do I do with this information and how do I use it?"

Chapter 3 – The Vocation of Being Human: We All Have Needs
Our fallen natures combined with influences from a fallen world exert a distorting influence upon our *beliefs* regarding how our *needs* can be met and *desires* fulfilled. Restoration and renewal of broken spiritual hearts begins with the foundational and interrelated complex of *needs, desires,* and *beliefs.* The *beliefs* that we have internalized through conscious choice or through non-conscious influences (other people, culture, media messaging, etc.) regarding how our *needs* can be met are the central-most component of the spiritual heart and the central-most issue in our spiritual walk as believers in the all-sufficient work of Jesus our Lord (e.g. Rom 12:2; Eph 4:17–31).

Chapter 4 – Behaviors: Portals of Insight into Flourishing or Failing
Have you wanted to understand the root causes for flourishing or failing? *Behaviors* provide portals or windows into our spiritual hearts—measures of flourishing or failing. Internalized *belief*s, *belief systems*, and *behaviors* form the basis for habituation of patterns that become our persona, our identity. Suffering is inevitable in this life. God allows it. He uses that suffering to effect transformation of habituated patterns and identities in us so that we may become more conformed to His image. The impact of suffering can stimulate us to examine any false *beliefs* which underlie habituated *behaviors*—even those which are unconscious to us. Restoration and renewal of the spiritual heart requires identifying *behaviors* and the *belief systems* which support them. *Behaviors* provide portals into the *beliefs* and *belief systems* which are the root of our flourishing or failing in our lives.

Chapter 5 – Strongholds - Fortifications in the Spiritual Heart
What happens when we reinforce our beliefs by repeating the same *behaviors* over and over again? In this chapter, we look at Paul's statements about strongholds in his letter to the Corinthians. He equates spiritual heart strongholds to "arguments and every lofty opinion raised against the knowledge of God" (2 Cor 10:5 ESV).

We examine how habituation of *behaviors* form strongholds and why they are detrimental to our spiritual hearts. Finally, I describe how we destroy these fortifications. Stronghold fortifications must be destroyed if our hearts are to be aligned to God's heart.

Chapter 6 – Who We Were, Who We Are, and Who We Can Be
In their hit release single, "Redeemed," Big Daddy Weave sings of not being who he used to be. On the one hand, we have been redeemed; on the other hand, our fallen nature leaves us with a problematic dichotomy. Who we were, who we are, and who we can be is the dynamic through which we must navigate until the day we die. In chapter 6, we explore the phrase "old self" which encapsulates the anthropocentric orientation of the *beliefs, expectations*, and *behavior* complex of the spiritual heart. The phrase "new self" encapsulates the God glorifying orientation of the components of the spiritual heart. If we grasp the significance of the meaning of these phrases, we grasp what will be vital to understanding the spiritual heart condition and solution process—who we were, who we are, and who we can be.

Chapter 7 – The Best Helper
In chapter 7, we dispense with the notion of passively expecting a supernatural experience to transcend our spiritual hearts into a new realm. We are active participants, but we have a divine Helper. The transformation and renewal of our minds infuses the character of God into our spiritual hearts which is made manifest in observable ways known as the fruit of the Spirit (Gal 5:22–24). The Holy Spirit ministers to us, but spiritual heart transformation leads to filling with the character of God. Unrealistic *expectations* regarding the "filling with the Holy Spirit" leave us adrift on the sea of notions without a rudder and without direction. We have the best Helper.

Chapter 8 – When Hearts Align
In chapter 8, we address the "how." The apostle Paul defines a process that will lead to the transformation of the spiritual heart into conformity with the image of Christ. The character of God and Christ is infused as we put off the "old self" and put on the "new self" following Paul's process. The process of the alignment of our hearts to God's heart will not be smooth. It is messy because we are imperfect and we live in an imperfect world.

Introduction

What if we learned early in our lives the key to understanding people—why people behave the way they do, what motivates them, what makes them tick. What if we learned early in life the same about ourselves? Would it change the way we engaged with others? Would it have changed the way we viewed ourselves? Would it even have changed decisions we made and the course of our lives?

I sometimes wonder what my life might have looked like had I known as a youngster what I know now. The apostle Paul's encouragement to the Philippians to keep pressing forward rather than looking back (Phil 3:13) encourages me. But if I could have chosen one truth to have understood at a much earlier age, it would be the model for evaluating the spiritual heart I present in this book.

The adolescent and teenage years of our lives are an awkward period. It's normal for those years to be awkward. (I wish I had known then that "awkward" was the norm.) I held beliefs about myself and others built upon some degree of insecurity, doubtless influenced by some of the insecurities of my family members. My father was extremely hard working and dedicated to his family. And he was a disciplinarian. Yet, his area of insecurity related to his lack of education. For some reason that I never have been able to determine, he was removed from school in the second grade and spent his early years as the child who worked the fields and tended to the chickens, firewood, and other subsistence farming efforts. That absence of education left a deep mark on his spiritual heart.

Among several incidents that revealed the wound to me, was a time when I was nine or ten years old and my dad and I were sitting in a men's group meeting at the small Methodist church we attended. The men sat in a circle. They started reading verses of the Bible in turn. And my dad's turn came. He pretended to be unable to read without his glasses and asked to pass. One man actually offered to give my dad his glasses, and my dad pretended the prescription was incorrect. I was angry. Why would these men embarrass another man like that? My dad!

Shame! Feelings of inferiority! It is difficult to describe the depth of such a wound to the spiritual heart. Imagine being told at a young age that you cannot learn by adults! Once that belief is internalized, it is compounded and reinforced over time. I absorbed some of his social insecurities and it took years to resolve those. I swore I would never allow myself to be in that position. I determined to get an education, no matter what. In my spiritual heart, I had just begun constructing my own defense mechanism against the pain I saw. I pursued education motivated as much as by pain management as by a desire to learn.

When I became a Christian in my teens, I did not immediately have the answers to how to orient my spiritual heart to God's heart. I was just trying to navigate life like everyone else. I envisioned success as getting an education so I could get a job. I learned hard work from my dad, and during my first two years of college, I made straight A's. Who does that while also having a social life? Well, no one I knew – including me.

Was I a Christian? Yes. Did my life look anything like what God desired for me and my spiritual heart? Did it resemble His heart? Was it what we might consider to have been healthy? Not really. God desires our hearts to be restored, redeemed, made whole.

Had I understood the truths in this book, perhaps I could have had a redemptive influence in the lives of others, even my dad. Maybe I could have spoken into his heart words to encourage and uplift him based upon an understanding of the deepest needs that he had—needs that were never met. He held beliefs about himself and he spent his life fighting against those beliefs and never found the complete answer. I wonder what I could have said that might have changed the lies he'd accepted. Don't get me wrong. He accomplished a lot worthy of a book of its own and I have wonderful and bright memories of him, things we did, and things he taught me, but the wounds festered until the day he died. Little did I know then, but his wounds were also my wounds to a degree.

What about all the other kids with whom I grew up? Every one of them had their own wounds. I saw the effect of the injuries in their lives, but did not understand their causes. What about my troops when I was a Marine officer? What about my co-workers in business? My dates when I was dating? My family? My wife? In every category and case, spiritual hearts of people are in need of restoration and renewal—even those who had "perfect" families.

What about you? And the people in your sphere of influence?

The Bible gives us a model that can guide us through exploring the complexities of the spiritual heart and engaging in redemptive discussions and relationships, just as Jesus would do.

Chapter 1 – Our Greatest Need: Congruent Hearts Aligned with God's Heart

Consider John and Trish, a Christian couple (fictional names and a composite story). Trish decides to leave John after twenty years of marriage. The two teenage children followed their mother. John is bitter and angry at everyone, including God, over the injustice he has suffered. When John married Trish, John believed that Trish would fill the hole in his heart of his need for companionship, love, acceptance, respect, approval, and so many other needs including physical. He believed that Trish had the same values and expectations of marriage that he had: blue-collar values within a white-collar, professional, career-oriented home and neighborhood—all supported by John's income while Trish focused on the children. John and Trish both came from dysfunctional families. John's dad was largely out of the picture in John's life. He worked in the construction industry at out-of-state job sites. When John's father was home, his drinking led to his parent's divorce when John was only thirteen. Trish's parents stayed together but it was anything but a happy union. Her dad was a lawyer and provided well, but he was verbally abusive, and Trish's mom tried to keep the peace. Once Trish and her siblings went off to college, Trish's mom became consumed in her arts and crafts business, mainly to escape the emptiness of her family life. Trish's mom instilled in her daughters the need to be financially independent from a husband, mainly based upon her experience.

At first, John and Trish felt content in their marriage, and it seemed to align with their expectations. Having married young, Trish gave birth to two healthy children within a year of each other. The first ten years seemed great. John advanced in his law firm to senior partner. Yet, below the surface, Trish had needs and desires which went unmet. She wanted more. As a "creative type," friends at a large advertising agency encouraged her to join them. After three years enjoying her own career, Trish found that she and John had become emotionally and physically distant. Trish felt trapped, and the marriage dissolved.

John's heart is broken. He has concluded that, for some reason, God brought this suffering into his life to punish him. He cannot identify a specific reason for the punishment, but the injustice of it all doesn't align with what he believed about God's love—especially how God supposedly loves him.

Now, John attends your church. Trish stayed with the church in which they had raised the two children. John even feels abandoned by his former church and his children. John asks you to help him. Where do you begin? How do you navigate through a spiritual heart which is so broken?

We Have a Heart Problem

Humans suffer from a heart problem. Heart disease and strokes, when combined, lead in the causes of death in the United States.[1] However, humans suffer from a much more pervasive and insidious *spiritual* heart disease, more impactful than cardiovascular disease, a physical ailment. Spiritual heart disease is invisible, immaterial, yet visible in terms of its effects. The God of all creation highly values the invisible, immaterial, spiritual heart of humankind. He provides a means for its restoration and renewal.

The voices and lives of the people with whom I have engaged over the years demands a biblical model that will allow us to objectively exam our lives and the way we engage with others.

---

[1] Melonie Heron, Ph.D., Division of Vital Statistics, "Deaths: Leading Causes for 2017," *National Vital Statistics Reports* 68, no. 6 (June 24, 2019): 17, https://www.cdc.gov/nchs/data/nvsr/nvsr68/nvsr68_06-508.pdf.

The model should help us move toward non-destructive, healthy, redemptive, and supportive interactions and relationships with others. Simply put, we must be enabled to make sense of the mess of any personal brokenness in our lives, the lives of others, and the world at large—brokenness due to our fallen state as descendants of Adam and Eve plus our own personal sins and the sins of others. This renewal-restoration is a process—not a one-time event or a transaction. Successful engagement in this process requires an understanding of the spiritual heart from a biblical perspective.

The Word "Heart" Appears 757 Times in 706 Verses

The number of times the word "heart" appears in the Bible demands our attention. We find the Greek word for heart (*kardia*) and its related forms in the New Testament 156 times in 149 verses.[2] We find the Hebrew word for heart (*lev*) and its related forms 601 times in 557 verses in the Old Testament.[3] A combined

---

[2] Michael W. Holmes, *The Greek New Testament: SBL Edition* (Lexham Press; Society of Biblical Literature, 2011-2013) search results for καρδια using Logos Bible Software, version 8.14.

[3] *The Lexham Hebrew Bible* (Bellingham, WA: Lexham Press, 2012) search results for לֵב using Logos Bible Software, version 8.14.

total of 757 times in the sixty-six books of the Bible should alert even the most casual reader.

The overwhelming majority of these uses refer to a non-physical, spiritual entity—not the physical muscle just to the left of center in a human's chest—the basis of physical life and the proximate cause of so many deaths each year. God must consider the spiritual heart of humans an important subject to have referenced it in such a prominent and frequent manner in the Bible.

God Has a Spiritual Heart and Humans Have the Imago Dei

The Bible indicates that God Himself possesses a spiritual heart. In Genesis 6:6, we read that God experienced grief or offense in **His heart** due to the wickedness that spread throughout the earth just prior to the judgment of the Flood. In Genesis 8:21, just after Noah exits the ark and offers animal sacrifices to God, the Lord takes notice of Noah's offering and promises in **His heart** that He will never again curse the ground and destroy everything that lives. In 1 Samuel 2:35, God promises to raise up a faithful priest in Israel who acts according to **God's heart**—not like the sons of Eli the priest who abused the power of their office. Slightly later in the narrative God expresses his displeasure with Saul due to his unfaithfulness and disobedience (1 Sm 13:14). He selects a replacement—a man after **God's own heart**. God desired a man whose spiritual heart was in alignment with **God's heart**.

God created the first humans as His image (Ge 1:26). The non-material, non-physical, spiritual heart of the first humans reflected the spiritual heart of their Maker. There was alignment. After the Fall in the Garden, humans still possessed incredible vestiges of the *imago dei* (image of God) including the spiritual heart. Among the many problems injected into God's perfect creation by the Fall was the misalignment between God's heart and the spiritual heart of the man and the woman.

This Truth Impacts Lives

The profundity of this truth impacts lives. You impact every person with whom you cross paths based upon how you impact their spiritual heart—the part of a human which God values immensely. We can impact people's spiritual hearts positively or negatively, beneficially or destructively, every day. Others have impacted and will impact your spiritual heart—in helpful ways in some cases and in destructive ways in others.

The philosophies of entire societies are shaped by the acceptance or rejection of this truth—the truth that the spiritual hearts of the first humans reflected God's image, God's spiritual heart—the truth that the vestige of that image (the imago dei) has resided in humans since the Fall. Philosophies, ideologies, and belief systems of societies which recognize this truth place a high value upon the dignity and worth of an individual. Conversely, collectivist ideologies tend to devalue the individual in the interest of the "greater good." Jesus died to provide individuals an opportunity to be restored and renewed should individuals accept His free gift. Why? Because God places a high value upon the spiritual heart of each individual human. When this truth is understood and embraced by a people, it influences people's behaviors toward others—individually and as a society.

The Bible Affirms God's High Valuation of the Spiritual Heart

God cares about the spiritual heart immensely. He sent His Son to pay the penalty of sin as a consequence of the Fall in the

Garden of Eden—an event with profound impact upon the human spiritual heart. If we choose to accept it, Jesus' work on the Cross provides each of us with eternal life *and* the potential for renewal and restoration of our broken spiritual hearts—brokenness resulting from the ravages and effects of sin in our lives and the lives of others.

The frequent references to the spiritual heart in Scripture cry out for our attention. The reality of this phenomenon impacted me only in recent years. Down deep, I had heard and could repeat definitions or descriptions of the spiritual heart such as "the innermost part of man" or "your inner being"—definitions which created more questions than they answered. Eventually, I tossed such amorphous definitions into the category of "fortune cookie theology", a category in which I place statements made in churches and Christian circles which really amount to broad and meaningless notions. Such terms and phrases always left me with the impression that—"they must know something I don't know."

God does not leave us to float on a proverbial "sea of notions" with a false belief that someday we might somehow drift and make landfall on the "shore of clarity."

God values the spiritual heart too much to leave us with nothing but a fog of notions. His Word provides us with guidance to steer us to the shore of clarity.

References to the Spiritual Heart in the Old Testament

In Genesis 6:5, the wickedness of humans, a reflection of their spiritual heart, prompted God to pronounce and execute the judgment of the Flood. The rejection of God's revealed truth and the false beliefs of that generation's hearts caused them to reject the opportunity to join Noah and his family in the ark of God's provision. Thousands of years later, Exodus 7:13 informs us regarding the hardened nature of Pharaoh's "heart." Bad things always attend a hardened heart. In both cases, spiritual hearts full of unbelief led to the documented drownings of an army for all of history to observe. Beliefs (and unbeliefs) have consequences.

Paul addresses the rejection of God's revelation and truth in Romans 1:18–32 and references these prior generations. Paul highlights idolatry and behaviors contrary to God's design for interpersonal relationships and interactions among humans. Within that section of Romans 1, Paul notes in verse 21 that "...*they became futile in their thinking, and their foolish hearts were darkened.*" In verse 24, he notes that "...*God gave them up in the lusts of their hearts.*" In verse 25, Paul adds that "...*they exchanged the truth about God for a lie.*"[4] In Ephesians 4:18, Paul instructs his readers to live no longer as those who "...*are darkened in their understanding, alienated from the life of God because of the ignorance that is in them, due to their hardness of heart.*"

We also observe the heart associated with terms such as spirit, soul, emotions, thought, beliefs, expectations, desires, one's bodily needs, one's conscience, motivations and many different categories and types of behaviors. Genesis 42:28 indicates that the hearts of Joseph's brothers "failed them" when they discovered that

---

[4] All Scripture quotations designated (ESV) are from the *ESV Bible* (Wheaton, Illinois: Crossway, 2008).

they might be accused of theft. One of them discovered his money had been returned secretly to his belongings as they left Egypt. They were returning to their father, so they could have been accused of theft. We cannot help but observe the close association between their emotions, conscience, and expectations with their spiritual hearts in this narrative. Their spiritual hearts are laden with guilt over their past as they live with the constant expectation of God's punishment for what they did to their younger brother. Their lives are negatively impacted by the brokenness within their spiritual hearts.

In Deuteronomy 4:29, Moses instructs the Israelites. He informs them of the consequences of covenant disobedience—discipline and punishment. However, repentance leads to blessing. When scattered among the nations due to their disobedience, the Lord could be found if they sought Him with all their *heart* and *soul*.

The spiritual heart and soul are closely linked in Scripture. Psalm 20:4 ("May He grant your heart's desire…") establishes an association of the spiritual heart with *desires*. Romans associates the spiritual heart with the *conscience* in 2:15, with one's *desires* in 10:1 and with one's *beliefs* in 10:9–10. Scripture overflows with associations of the spiritual heart to other immaterial aspects of our being and our *behaviors*.

When we consider the additional references in Scripture to the immaterial, spiritual heart, we have a more comprehensive platform of observations to help biblically define this thing called the heart. In Genesis, we observe the immaterial, spiritual heart of humans in association with *intentions* and *thoughts* (Ge 6:5; 8:21); *self-talk* (Ge 17:17; 24:45); *integrity* (Ge 20:5–6); and *fear* (Ge 42:28). Exodus documents Pharaoh's *hardened heart* (Ex 4:21; 7:3, 13, 22; 8:15, 22, 32; 9:7, 12, 35; 10:1, 20, 27; 11:10; 14:4, 8) and the heart motivates *acts of financial generosity* (Ex 25:2; 35:22, 26, 29).

In Deuteronomy, had the hearts of the Israelites contained *beliefs* consistent with God's purposes for them as a people (Dt 10:15), they would have been motivated to act as encouraged by God. Their hearts would have aligned with God's heart. This alignment would have been manifested by such things as…

† Seeking the Lord (Dt 4:29).

† Loving the Lord and keep His commandments (Dt 6:5; 26:16).

† Avoiding self-righteousness (Dt 8:14, 17; 9:4–5).

- † Remembering and passing on to subsequent generations all that God had done (Dt 4:9; 30:2; 32:46).
- † Not being fearful of other nations (Dt 1:28; 7:17; 20:3, 8).
- † Passing God's tests designed to reveal the condition of their hearts (Dt 8:2, 5; 13:3; 28:47).
- † Turning not to other gods (Dt 11:16; 29:18; 30:17).
- † Showing financial compassion to the poor among them (Dt 15:7, 9–10).
- † Israel's kings would not accumulate wealth and riches at the expense of the people (Dt 17:17, 20).
- † Avoiding succumbing to self-deception (Dt 29:19).
- † Enjoying hope in the promises of future blessing, especially when repentance occurred (Dt 30:2, 6, 10, 14).

If the Israelites failed to orient their spiritual hearts to God's purposes and desires for them as demonstrated by their faith through obedience, then insecurity and a withholding of God's promised blessings awaited them (Dt 28:65, 67; 29:4). Deuteronomy connects the spiritual heart to *beliefs, values, expectations, emotions, and behaviors*—all of which God observes and which becomes the basis of blessing or discipline for the Israelites.

References to the heart pour from the pages of the wisdom literature in Scripture. Consider the following examples of activities and descriptions attributed to the spiritual heart.

- † Meditation (the formation and internalization of *beliefs*) occurs within the heart (Ps 4:4; 77:6).
- † The heart is the locus of *emotions and behaviors* such as worship, joy, praise, and communion with God which emanate from *beliefs* (Ps 4:7; 13:5; 16:9; 19:8, 14, 22:26; 27:8: 28:7; 33:21; 40:8; 44:18; 45:1; 49:3; 57:7; 62:8; 64:10; 69:32; 84:2; 86:11; 97:11; 105:3; 108:1).
- † The heart is the locus of God's testing of *beliefs* and *expectations* (Ps 7:9; 17:3; 26:2; 78:8; 107:12).
- † The whole heart is involved in the *behavior* of giving thanks, seeking the Lord, and observing His laws (Ps 9:1; 86:12; 111:1; 119:2, 10, 34, 69, 145; 138:1).
- † The heart is the locus of courage founded in *beliefs* and *behaviors* (Ps 10:6, 17; 27:3; 31:24).
- † The heart is the locus of self-deception due to mental *behaviors* such as rationalization, justification and self-deceit (Ps 10:11, 13; 14:1; 33:25; 53:1).

- † The heart is the locus of the believer's alignment to God's righteousness as manifested by *behaviors* (Ps 11:2; 15:2; 16:7; 24:4; 27:14; 32:11; 36:10; 37:31; 51:6, 10; 73:1, 13, 21, 26; 84:5; 90:12; 94:15; 101:2; 112:7–8; 119:7, 11, 80, 111–112, 145, 161; 125:4).

- † A double heart / divided heart is one that waivers between *beliefs* and *values* (Ps 12:2; 28:3; 55:21).

- † The heart is the locus of the *emotions* of sorrow and brokenness due to unmet *expectations* (Ps 13:2; 25:17; 38:8; 39:3; 40:12; 51:17; 69:20; 89:50; 94:19; 102:4; 109:22).

- † The heart can be closed or hardened in *unbelief* and arrogance (Ps 17:10; 36:1; 55:15; 78:18, 37; 81:12; 95:8, 10; 101:4, 5; 131:1).

- † The heart is the locus of fear due to *unbelief* (Ps 18:45; 38:10; 55:4; 61:2; 143:4).

- † The heart is related to *desires* and plans/*expectations* (Ps 20:4; 21:2; 37:4; 41:6; 58:2; 62:10; 73:7; 140:2; 141:4).

- † The Lord's heart is reflected in His plans/*expectations* and actions/*behaviors* (Ps 33:11; 78:72).

† The heart is the focus of God's attention – what God values (Ps 33:15; 44:21; 64:6; 66:18; 139:23).

† The heart is the locus of wisdom and understanding (*beliefs*)– thus, the basis for a life of flourishing (Prv 2:2, 10; 3:5; 4:21; 7:3; 11:29; 14:30, 33; 15:15; 16:21; 18:15; 22:17; 23:12, 15; 27:9; 31:11).

† The heart houses *beliefs* that translate into decisions and plans/*expectations* of man (Prv 3:1; 4:4; 6:21; 7:25; 12:23; 14:14; 15:13; 16:1, 9; 19:3, 18; 20:9; 27:19; 29:17).

† The heart is the center of *motivation* and direction (Prv 3:3; 12:25; 13:12; 23:19, 26).

† God encourages integrity of heart, i.e. no incongruous *beliefs* and no incongruity between *beliefs* and *behaviors* (Prv 3:5; 4:23; 26:23, 24, 25).

† A humble and teachable heart mitigates against regrets arising from the inevitable unmet *expectations* associated with *beliefs* not aligned to truth (Prv 5:12; 10:8; 15:14; 18:12).

† The spiritual heart of the "worthless person" translates *beliefs* into *behaviors* harmful to others—a "heart" that is

listed among seven things the Lord hates (Prv 6:14, 18; 7:10; 12:20; 15:7; 23:7; 24:2).

- † The heart of the righteous contrasts with the heart of the wicked person as evidenced by the different *behaviors* and underlying *beliefs* (Prv 10:20; 11:20; 15:28; 23:17; 28:14).
- † The heart can conceal what one chooses not to disclose because of what we *believe* and *expect* others may think or do (Prv 14:10, 13; 20:5; 25:3).
- † God knows, tests and exposes the heart, especially the proud and arrogant heart which has embraced *beliefs* not aligned with God's truth (Prv 15:11; 16:15; 17:3; 21:1, 2, 4; 22:15; 24:12).
- † The heart oriented to truth-based *beliefs* and *values* produces *emotions* of joy, happiness and enjoyment in contrast to a crushed spirit (Prv 15:30; 17:22; 25:20).
- † The wise of heart exercises prudence and judiciousness in speech, a *behavior*, in contrast to the unwise (Prv 16:23; 17:20; 22:11; 23:33; 24:17; 27:11).
- † The heart is the locus of intention/*expectations*, decision, *motivation* and *desire* (Eccl 1:13; 2:22).

- † The heart is the locus of self-talk and inner reflection—mental *behaviors* (Eccl 1:16; 2:1, 3, 15; 3:17-18; 7:1-5, 22; 9:1).
- † The heart acquires and houses wisdom and knowledge (Eccl 1:13, 16, 17; 7:25; 8:5, 9; 8:16)—descriptions of *internalized beliefs* and *values* aligned with truth.
- † The heart is the locus of pleasure and joy as related to *desires*—whether rightly aligned to truth principles or not (Eccl 2:10; 5:20; 9:7; 11:9).
- † The heart is the locus of despair due to unmet *desire* and unmet *expectations* (Eccl 2:20, 23).
- † God places a sense of eternity in the heart (Eccl 3:11).
- † Prayer emerges from the spiritual heart (Eccl 5:2).
- † When one's focus is upon satisfying *desires*, the spiritual heart corrupts (Eccl 7:7).
- † Anger arising from unmet *expectations* lodges in the heart of a fool (Eccl 7:9).
- † What others say can influence the *beliefs* and related behaviors of the *heart* (Eccl 7:21, 26).
- † A delay of justice can influence the *beliefs* and related *behaviors* of the heart (Eccl 8:11).

- † The spiritual heart houses "evil" and "madness" (Eccl 9:3)—*beliefs* not aligned to truth.
- † The heart of the wise and of the fool are diametrically opposed (Eccl 10:2).
- † Vexation occurs in the heart (Eccl 11:10).

The wisdom books of the Hebrew Scriptures also illustrate the linkage of the spiritual heart to *desires, beliefs, expectations, motivations,* and *behaviors*. All of these references so far have been from the 39 books of the Old Testament, or as I prefer to refer to them, the Hebrew Scriptures in honor of our Jewish friends. What about the New Testament?

References to the Spiritual Heart in the First Century Scriptures

As I have previously noted, the First Century Scriptures contain numerous references to the spiritual heart as well—156 times in 149 verses. A fairly representative sample follows.

- † Blessings arise from a "pure" heart (Mt 5:8; Jn 7:38).
- † Sin originates in the heart *motivated* by incorrect beliefs (Mt 5:28; Lk 21:34; Jn 13:2).

- † We attach the focus of our hearts upon what we highly value—mostly how we and others satisfy our *needs* and *desires* (Mt 6:21; Lk 12:34).

- † We experience encouragement in our spiritual hearts (Mt 9:2, 22; 14:27; Mk 6:50; 10:49; Lk 18:1; Jn 14:27; 16:22, 33).

- † Evil thinking (*beliefs* and *values*) occurs in the heart and gives rise to wrong *behavior* (Mt 9:4; 15:19; Mk 7:21; Lk 1:51).

- † An attitude of service to others (a *value*) emanates from the spiritual heart (Mt 11:29).

- † Our speech and words (*behaviors*) emerge from and reflect the heart (Mt 12:34; 15:18; Lk 6:45).

- † Sensitivity to spiritual truth (a reflection of *values*) is the measure of the spiritual heart (Mt 13:15; Acts 28:27; Eph 4:18; 1 Jn 3:17).

- † Volitional changes and repentance (change of *beliefs* and adjustment of *expectations*) occur in the heart (Mt 13:15; Lk 1:17; Jn 12:40; Acts 28:27; Rom 10:9-10; 2 Cor 6:11, 13; 7:2; Eph 1:18).

- *Beliefs* are cycled and replaced within the spiritual heart (Mt 13:19; Lk 8:12).
- The spiritual heart can house *beliefs* and *behavior* patterns at odds with each other—sometimes referred to as cognitive dissonance in modern parlance (Mt 15:8; Mk 7:6).
- Forgiveness of others (a *value* and an *expectation*) occurs in the heart (Mt 18:35).
- The heart can be hardened with the acceptance of false or wrong *beliefs* to be true (Mt 19:8; Mk 3:5; 6:52; 8:17; 10:5; 16:14; Jn 12:40).
- We love the Lord God with heart, soul and mind (Mt 22:37; Mk 12:30, 33; Lk 10:27; 24:32).
- Doubt, questioning, and *unbelief* arise in the heart (Mk 2:6, 8; 11:23; Lk 5:22; 24:25, 38).
- The heart collects memories for future reflection and *belief* adjustment (Lk 1:66; 2:19, 51).
- Responses to events reveal the thoughts and *beliefs* of the heart (Lk 2:35; 9:47; Jn 16:6).
- A good heart is a storage of internalized *beliefs* (Lk 8:15).
- God knows and *values* the heart and bases His evaluation upon the heart (Lk 16:15; Jn 12:40; Acts 1:24; 8:21–22;

15:8; Rom 2:5; 8:27; 1 Cor 4:5; 14:25; 2 Cor 5:12; 1 Thes 2:4; 1 Pt 3:4; 1 Jn 3:20–21).

† The spiritual heart experiences encouragement as *expectations* are adjusted (Acts 2:26, 46; 14:17; 27:22, 25; 2 Cor 4:16; Eph 3:13; Col 2:2; 4:8).

† The heart includes the conscience or *values* (Acts 2:37; Rom 2:15).

† *Beliefs* held in common provide a source of agreement, cooperation and encouragement between people (Acts 4:32; Phlm 1:7).

† The *desires, beliefs, expectations,* and *behaviors* that emanate from the heart can be aligned to Satan's purposes and/or against God's desires (Acts 5:3–4; 7:39, 51; Rom 1:24; Jas 3:14; 2 Pt 2:14).

† The heart is the locus of intention, *motivation, desire,* and purpose (Acts 7:23; Rom 10:1, 8; 1 Cor 7:37; 2 Cor 9:7; Eph 6:5–6; Col 3:22–23; 2 Thes 3:5).

† Faith and righteousness (truth–based *beliefs* and *values*) produce a clean, pure and guarded heart (Acts 15:9; Phil 4:7; 1 Tm 1:5; 2 Tm 2:22; Jas 4:8).

† God opens the heart, establishes the heart as blameless, and comforts it (Acts 16:14; 1 Thes 3:13; 2 Thes 2:17; Phlm 1:12, 20). *Expectations* align to God's purposes, plans, and timing.

† The *emotions* associated with physical and/or spiritual separation from loved ones results in heart break (Acts 21:13; Rom 9:2; 2 Cor 2:4).

† The heart appreciates those whom one loves (2 Cor 7:3; 8:16; Eph 6:22; Phil 1:17; 1 Pt 1:22). Appreciation is a combination of *beliefs* and *values*.

† The rejection of God and truth (*unbelief*) darkens and makes foolish the spiritual heart (Rom 1:21).

† A spiritual heart that lacks compassion (a *value*, *emotion*, and *behavior* combined) lacks faith and the heart possessing compassion possesses faith (Rom 1:31; 2 Tm 3:3 cf. 2 Cor 3:2–3; Col 3:12; 1 Pt 3:8).

† The *beliefs* within the spiritual heart of the true Jew *motivated* observance of the Mosaic Law (Rom 2:29; 2 Cor 3:15).

- † The Holy Spirit ministers to the spiritual heart resulting in *beliefs*, *values*, *emotions*, and *behavioral* alignment (Rom 5:5; 2 Cor 1:22; Gal 4:6).
- † Obedience results when the *beliefs* within the spiritual heart synchronize with truth and related *behaviors* (Rom 6:17).
- † Internal self-talk and worship (*behaviors*) occurs in and emanates from the heart (Rom 10:6; Eph 5:19).
- † Deception (*belief* in a lie) finds a home in the spiritual heart of the naïve (Rom 16:18; Jas 1:26).
- † The spiritual heart envisions with *expectations* (1 Cor 2:9).
- † Inner peace (*expectations* aligned to truth) enjoys presence in the spiritual heart (Col 3:15).
- † Corporate praise and worship (behavior) emanate from the collective spiritual heart of believers (Col 3:16; 1 Pt 3:5).

What Do These Observations About the Spiritual Heart Tell Us?

These observations provide us with a lot of information about the spiritual heart. Even if you only scanned this compilation of references and associations of the heart in Scripture, the scope, breadth, and magnitude is phenomenal. The awe-inspiring nature of the spiritual heart can be compared to viewing the Milky Way from the vantage point of a 12,000 foot mountain peak in the Rocky Mountains on a cold, clear, winter's night. If you have ever had that or a similar experience viewing the vastness of Space illuminated by more stars than can possibly be counted, you have a good analogy for the significance of the spiritual heart.

Based upon these observations, the Bible presents the human spiritual heart as the whole of a person—*beliefs and values, expectations, emotions, motives, behaviors*—even the body, soul, and spirit. *Beliefs* are the central-most component of the spiritual heart of humans. Clearly, God values and desires that the spiritual heart of humans align to His heart. Beliefs and belief systems which are misaligned to truth misalign with God's heart. The spiritual heart of the human is the spiritual battlefield.

Synonyms for the Heart in Scripture

The synonyms in Scripture for the spiritual heart include the "*spirit of man*" (Prv 20:27; Eccl 3:21; Zec 12:1); "*man's spirit*" (Prv 18:14); "*inner parts…inmost self*" (Ps 5:9; Is 16:11); "*inner being*"

(Rom 7:22; Eph 3:16); and *"inner self"* (2 Cor 5:16). These synonyms are a part of a definition of the spiritual heart.

Toward the Shore of Clarity

Is there a way to define and describe the non-physical, spiritual heart that navigates us through the proverbial sea of notions toward the shore of clarity? Can we define the heart with greater specificity than such amorphous phrases as one's innermost being? Can we avoid conflating the spiritual heart with certain of its manifestations such as emotions or desires thereby misinterpreting and improperly defining it? Does a framework or model exist that enables us to engage in critical thinking about our spiritual hearts?

As a first step in our journey, we must understand what is broken and why. The biblical foundation for a restoration of spiritual heart health begins with grasping God's provision of a relationship with Him—Jesus and Jesus' work on the Cross to satisfy God's righteous requirements. We accept His free gift of His righteousness through faith. We completely surrender the false notion (*belief*) that whatever good we produce requires the great paternal being in the sky to accept us. We embrace the fact of our hopelessness and lack of any means to satisfy God apart from Jesus. We surrender any false notions of goodness or accomplishments relative to other fallen humans. We surrender any false notions that our fallen nature and past actions (including harm to others) may prevent God from working a work of redemption and restoration in our lives.

Once we accept Jesus' death as the basis for the payment of the penalty of sin and its validation through the resurrection, we receive the gift of God's righteousness. Yet, for most of us, after that point in our lives on this earth, many years remain to be lived in this fallen world. Even though we possess God's righteousness, we also possess spiritual hearts that have been damaged, or that are being damaged, by life in a fallen world. We live in a spiritual war zone. No one is immune from the impact upon the spiritual heart that living in a fallen world inflicts.

Christians engage in this war on the front line whether they realize it or not. Ill-equipped Christians suffer as perpetual casualties and wounded spiritual warriors. The battle rages inside of the spiritual heart and in the spiritual hearts of all of those who surround us. *Desires*, *beliefs*, *expectations*, and *behaviors* upon which we build our hopes and dreams shatter on the anvil of life in a fallen world with fallen people. Brokenness manifests itself not in physical loss of limbs like an earthly war, but through anxieties, addictions, personality disorders, false *beliefs* regarding our identity, abusive relationships, broken friendships, disappointments, failed *expectations*, and any number and combination of unmet *needs* and *desires* we seek to meet through other fallen humans.

You may ask—"Can these things really happen to people who have accepted God's gift and received His righteousness?" The answer—a resounding yes! In fact, to one degree or another, all of us suffer the wounds of this spiritual war—even those of us who accept the work of Jesus to have satisfied God's righteousness on our behalf. Christians must also answer the question of how to recover so the spiritual journey of our lives continue to advance toward the goal God has defined for us—a journey and goal of conformity to the image of Jesus (Rom 8:29), a goal which includes transformation by the renewal of our minds (Rom 12:2). Does the Bible contain instruction that provides us with hope?

Fortunately, hope exists. People with advanced degrees in psychology and counseling can provide help and insight into the identification and definition of problems; however, a degree in those specialties must be complemented with a biblically-based foundational understanding and model which can be repeatedly applied.

When I served in the military, the KISS principle—"keep it simple stupid"—got drilled into my head. I discovered profound wisdom in many of the military acronyms flooding my daily routines and "brain housing unit"—an affectionate term for our head. Seriously, when I first heard the acronym "KISS," I laughed inside and I am sure I valued it less than now. I found that those who truly grasp complex subjects are those who are able to reduce them to the greatest possible simplicity and clarity in their communications with others. Our complicated lives demand a simple model to help us define and understand this complex web of the spiritual heart. After all, our greatest need is for our hearts to align to God's heart.

Questions for Consideration:

† Can you think of any ways in which your spiritual heart is misaligned to God's heart? Do you have beliefs about your identity, purpose in life, and value which do not align with the way God sees and values you? Can you identify areas in which your spiritual heart needs renewal and restoration?

† Can you name three things you read in the lists of characteristics and descriptions of the spiritual heart in Scripture which you had not previously considered?

† What are some prevalent "notions" about the spiritual heart? Do they align with the Scriptural testimony?

Chapter 2 – Let's Begin with a Common Language

The Necessity of Defined Terminology and Concepts

Accountants, plumbers, electricians, attorneys, pilots, engineers, carpenters, programmers, military personnel, doctors, nurses and every profession known to humankind use specific terminology which must be understood by its practitioners. Have you ever thought where we would be if there was no consistency in the definitions of specific words, phrases, terms and concepts for our jobs? Would you feel confident in the cardiologist who told you that you have a problem with the "do-hickey" that fires electrical impulses to "some part of your heart" only to discover from your own research that you have a condition known as atrial fibrillation? Can you imagine the artillery fire direction officer giving a command to the battery to apply a certain deflection, angle, and charge to the howitzers and artillery rounds only to have everyone understand the terms however they thought appropriate? How about the controller with responsibility for the accounting close process each period who requests certain adjusting entries to specific accounts and the team just guesses what debits and credits to apply because they do not understand the nature of the accounts? What if pilots used different ways of measuring altitude and flew at whatever altitude their particular measure indicated? Wouldn't that be fun?

A Definition and Description of the Conceptual Components of the Spiritual Heart

Thankfully, we can only imagine such a dysfunctional world as would exist without technical and specifically defined vocabulary, phraseology, and concepts for each profession and endeavor of life. To the extent possible, we should have terminology and concepts to understand and communicate truth relative to such important biblical categories as the spiritual heart? Otherwise, we drift on a voyage to nowhere in particular on the proverbial sea of notions? Can we not at least establish anchor close to the shore of clarity? I believe we can. In fact, I think we can dock, disembark and explore? First, however, we must establish a working definition of the spiritual heart. I propose the following definition and brief description.

The phrase "spiritual heart" embraces the immaterial and material nature of humans. It is the repository of the *beliefs* and *values* which inform one's *expectations, emotions,* and observable *behaviors*. It represents the combined function of soul (eternal nature) and body (temporal nature).

I know that definition and description is loaded and needs to be unpacked. Let's attempt to do that. The definition attempts to provide us with a succinct statement of a much greater body of truth. As we unpack the definition, we will discover that it contains relevant and practical concepts to guide and frame critical thinking skills in our spiritual walk and heart function. The following drawing or diagram is a simple visual (remember KISS) that I use in the "unpacking." I have found that visuals serve to imprint the framework in our brains and provide a mental image to reference as we work through the concepts.

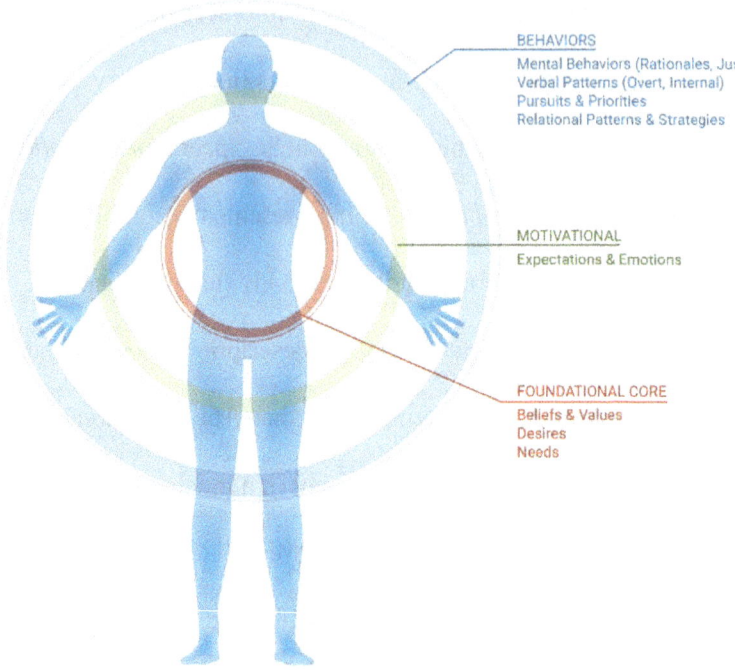

Needs, *desires*, and *beliefs and values* are foundational concepts to our understanding of the spiritual heart. All of the components of the spiritual heart revolve around the *beliefs* we accept to be true regarding how our *needs* can be met and *desires* fulfilled. Our *desires* to have our *needs* met drive our *motivations*. All *behaviors* are ultimately sourced from a *belief* or set of *beliefs*.

The category of *mental behaviors* includes the sub-categories of *rationales* and *justifications*. The root cause of our *behaviors* are traceable to the *beliefs* we have accepted either consciously or non-consciously.

Verbal behaviors are either *overt* (audible) or *internal* (non-audible). We constantly engage in self-talk. To prove the point, pause for a minute and focus upon what is going on in your mind. Did you notice your internal conversation? All of us are engaged in an internal conversation during all of our waking hours.

In the interest of simplicity, I have included *relational patterns* and *strategies* and *pursuits and priorities* without any sub-categories. The focus of this book is to ensure that a pliable, useable, and simple model is presented which can be used immediately by the reader.

Highly Integrated Components

In reality, these conceptual components function in a closely intertwined manner. Have you ever seen a tightly wound ball of rubber bands? Did you ever try to extract one of the rubber bands without also extracting several others? Any one of the rubber bands affects the integrity of the ball as a whole?

The rubber band ball illustrates the interrelationship between each of the components of the spiritual heart. All of the components of the spiritual heart interconnect and relate in the same way that the individual bands in the ball of rubber bands interconnect and relate with all others. A discussion of any one component of the spiritual heart in distinction from the other components is similar to attempting to extract one rubber band from the rubber band ball without affecting any other rubber bands.

In the Beginning…

Adam and Eve possessed legitimate God-given *needs* which intertwined with God-given *desires*. Their *beliefs and values, expectations* and *emotions* regarding how those *needs* and *desires* could be met and satisfied were simple. Initially, all of their *need*s, *desires, beliefs,* and *motives* perfectly aligned with God. He placed them in a paradise where their physical, emotional, intellectual, spiritual and relational *needs* paralleled perfect provision. The real potential existed to live forever in perfect fellowship with each other and their Creator—perfect harmony with a righteous Creator Who created perfect beings with no unrighteousness in them. They were created for a perfect environment. They believed that God had provided and would continue to provide for their every *need* UNTIL—Satan entered the picture disguised as a serpent.

The Fall in the Garden – The Consequences of Belief in Distorted Truth (Lies)

Satan, via the serpent, asked questions designed to sow seeds of doubt—*"Did God actually say…"* (Ge 3:1 ESV). Through this question, Satan induced Eve, then Adam who was with her, to not only question God's character and goodness, but to *believe* that God withheld something good from them—*"…for God knows that when you eat of it your eyes will be opened, and you will be like God, knowing good and evil"* (Ge 3:5 ESV).

In their deception, they accepted a false *belief*—a *belief* that God could not meet their *needs* nor satisfy their *desires*. They accepted the false *belief* that God had kept them from becoming wise and full of knowledge like Him. Of course, Satan failed to provide full disclosure of the consequences of disobeying God's one prohibition—the so-called "unintended consequences" of sin. Satan himself probably did not realize the full consequences of his fall and the fall of Adam and Eve. After all, Satan is not omniscient like God even though he is the most intelligent creature God created. Certainly, Adam and Eve did not realize the full consequences of their act of disobedience.

The acceptance of a false *belief* regarding the character, goodness, and love of God for Adam and Eve gave birth to *mental* and *verbal behaviors*. They engaged verbally with Satan and embraced the rationale he proposed. They *justified* their actions with the false *belief* that God had withheld something good from them. They *expected* a different outcome—one that would make them more like God rather than remove them from His presence.

Their *relational pattern* with God changed after they accepted the lie of Satan to be true. First, they avoided seeking the Lord and discussing Satan's proposal with Him, then they hid from

Him after their act of disobedience. Darkness flees from the light. They attempted to further *justify* themselves by covering themselves with fig leaves. Adam blamed Eve (Ge 3:12) and their *relational pattern* with each other (and God) was never the same.

Oh, what a tangled web we weave, what an intertwined and confused mess we make! Do you identify with what happened with Adam and Eve? Have you ever accepted a false *belief* (the lie) to be the truth? Have you found yourself in a sin pattern, a *behavior* pattern and realized that you had not considered whether it aligned with God's character and desires for you? Have you ever found yourself suffering from the unintended and unforeseen consequences of sin? If your answer to any of those questions is "yes," welcome to the human vocation?

Honesty with ourselves and God forces us to acknowledge that we've all been there—and some of us may still be to one extent or another. As we shall see, we acquire many of these *behavioral patterns* and the complex of *desires*, *beliefs*, *values*, *expectations*, and *emotions* that underpin them unconsciously. We then habituate their practice for so long that we are not even consciously aware of their existence. Many times, most times in fact, our unhappiness and suffering directly connects to *desires, beliefs*, *values*, *expectations, emotions, motivations,* and *behavior patterns* to which we've not given conscious thought.

Most know the story of Adam and Eve and many know that the Bible attributes the cause of humanity's unrighteous status before God to the fall in the Garden. However, what we so often miss is how this relates to our hearts and the brokenness in our lives and relationships. What *beliefs* have we accepted to be true about ourselves, others and God which are not true? How do we begin to understand and correct the impact of the false *beliefs* and lies we have accepted to be true—*beliefs* in lies which have had devastating impact upon our *expectations, relational behaviors,* our *internal self-talk* and our *pursuits* and *priorities*? That is the journey we will begin in the next few chapters.

Questions for Consideration:

† Are you able to identify a belief which you have accepted to be true regarding how your needs might be met, yet the belief is not based upon truth? As we shall see, we embrace beliefs regarding ourselves, our identity, how we should relate to others, and about every facet of life in this fallen world. The beliefs relate to our needs as humans. They can

be informed by truth or informed by a false perception, a lie.

† Can you provide an example of a belief you have unconsciously embraced from your culture?

Chapter 3 – The Vocation of Being Human: We All Have Needs

The phrase "spiritual heart" embraces the immaterial and material nature of humans. It is the repository of the *beliefs* and *values* which inform one's *expectations, emotions,* and observable *behaviors*. It represents the combined function of soul (eternal nature) and body (temporal nature).

We devote little conscious thought to our *needs*, yet our *desire* to have our *needs* met plays a dominating role in what *motivates* us. Throughout our lives, we form *beliefs* regarding how our *needs* can be met. The basis for all of our *behaviors* is the foundation consisting of the interwoven complex of our *needs, desires, beliefs, and values.*

As we have noted, it is difficult to analyze the components of the spiritual heart in isolation from each other. Like the individual bands in our rubber band ball analogy, they are simply too interrelated. Yet, as imperfect of a process as it may be, we can understand these terms and concepts individually and as they interrelate to each other. Together, they hold the key to our comprehension of the spiritual heart.

We Begin with Needs

Adam and Eve were created with legitimate *needs*. Yahweh made provision for their *needs* to be met in the perfect environment of the Garden and through each other in perfect relationship with a perfect God. They were created for perfect conditions. Of course, after the fall, everything got distorted. The first example of this was the attempt to cover their nakedness with fig leaves (Ge 3:7), a human-centered (anthropocentric) answer to a problem they created—a problem which only had a divine solution.

The spiritual heart of Adam and Eve designed for a perfect environment battled the stress and pressure of survival in an imperfect and fallen world. The theme of anthropocentricity and self-centered *beliefs* regarding how their *needs* could be met and *desires* fulfilled blossomed with plenty of thorns outside of the perfect Garden.

We often *believe* some things are a *need* which may not be a legitimate *need*. For instance, when Rick says "I *need* that car" and that car is a $150,000 sports car, Rick is probably conflating the word *"need"* with something much more than a *"need"*—unless of course Rick is a billionaire who has a car collection with a gap that only that car can fill. But, let's stick with the basic point of the analogy. For most people in this case, including Rick, a legitimate *need* for transportation has possibly been attached to *beliefs* regarding his status, his identity, a symbol, his acceptance in a certain group, the way he expects to relate to others, or any number of other *needs* and *desires*.

The perceived *"need"* for that car may *motivate* Rick to prioritize his time and energy to pursue more money to purchase it. Rick makes other lifestyle and *behavioral* changes in order to obtain this *desire* of his heart. Rick has *expectations* and *emotions* related to the car and all that he has connected to it. Eventually, through the habituation of *behaviors* associated with his *beliefs and expectations*, Rick has internalized everything connected to the attainment of his prized sports car. The car and all of the *beliefs* and *behaviors* associated with it have become Rick's identity.

Our fictional Rick is analogous to the fictional Gollum in the movie adaptation of J.R.R. Tolkien's *The Lord of the Rings*. Gollum referred to the ring as "my precious." I can still hear the hiss. The *beliefs*, *motivations*, and *behaviors* of Gollum in regard to the ring was his identity.

     I know. On the surface, my simple illustrations with Rick and Gollum may not adequately represent more complex scenarios. What about the false *beliefs* regarding how we define ourselves which result from past harms, injustices, wrongs, or sins of others (or ourselves) and which continue to dominate our *expectations*, *relations* with others, and other *behaviors* such as our patterns of *internal self-talk*? All we need to do is to substitute Rick's *desire* for the expensive sports car with any perceived *need* and *desire* we may have. Then, identify the *beliefs, expectations,* and all categories of *behavior* we associate with that need. Use some of the questions I suggest in this book as an aide. The answers will take you on a journey of discovery of your spiritual heart.

     For instance, do you associate your identity with a job, a career, a position, social circles, or any other thing people might perceive to represent "success?" Do you associate your identity with a past injustice, abuse, wrong, hurt, or any other experience that might have defined you in a negative way? All of these examples (and many more as we shall see shortly) are at odds with the identity in Christ we have as believers. Each of these examples are reflections of the *beliefs* we can embrace that are misaligned to truth. Each of these examples are reflections of *beliefs* regarding our *needs*. These *beliefs* drive our *behaviors* and impact our relations with others.

We live within and absorb from an increasingly idolatrous society and culture. No, I haven't seen any Baal worshippers recently, but here in the West, and particularly, here in the United States, our economy is consumption driven.[5] Many activities and *pursuits* are a legitimate part of a flourishing culture and society. However, even legitimate *pursuits* can become idolatrous when associated with the wrong *belief system*. For instance, prior to Covid-19, on any given weekend in the Fall through March of the following year, millions of Americans invested hundreds of hours watching and talking about football and basketball, collegiate and professional.

I enjoy college football and basketball. But, increasingly, I have had to step back and ask myself if I am using my time in a

---

[5] U.S. Bureau of Economic Analysis, Shares of gross domestic product: Personal consumption expenditures [DPCERE1Q156NBEA], retrieved from FRED, Federal Reserve Bank of St. Louis; https://fred.stlouisfed.org/series/DPCERE1Q156NBEA, June 9, 2020. The Federal Reserve Bank of St. Louis' chart of the trend of personal consumption expenditures relative to GDP discloses that consumer spending has risen relative to GDP from 58.6 percent at the end of Q1 1967 to 68.1 percent at the end of Q4 2019.

God-honoring way. For many people, shopping and buying to experience the adrenaline hit of a new pair of shoes, clothes, guns, or computer gear can become an idol if they are improperly connected to perceptions of *needs* and *beliefs* about our identity and priorities. None of these activities are inherently wrong. However, it is a truth that how you and I invest our time and money directly correlate to what we *value* within our *belief system*.

Albert Bandura developed a new behavioral theory of learning in the late 1970s called the Social Learning Theory. His theory is an attempt to describe how behavior is changed through observation. Social learning principles derived from Bandura's theory led the advertising industry to associate behaviors with the products promoted, thus encourage greater purchasing. If the potential purchaser wants the type of behavior on display, then he or she *needs* our product. Viewers and listeners more or less passively absorbed a *need* from culture. Bandura later became best known for his work on how television violence influenced *behaviors*.[6] More about *behaviors* in the next chapter, but these examples serve to

---

[6] William R. Yount, *Created to Learn: A Christian Teacher's Introduction to Educational Psychology* (Nashville, Tennessee: B&H Publishing, 2010), 222-23.

illustrate the highly intertwined nature of all of the components of the spiritual heart.

What are Needs?

What do we really *need* as humans? What are legitimate *needs*? Is it possible that one person may have *needs* that differ from those of another person? In the previous examples, we identified some common, legitimate *needs* which all humans possess. These needs often become intertwined and distorted when associated with *beliefs* and *motives* not aligned with truth principles.

In her book, *Five to Thrive: How to Determine if Your Core Needs are Being Met (And What to Do If They're Not,* Dr. Kathy Koch provides five questions to help her readers understand and define core *needs*. Prior to the fall in the Garden, the answers were on display daily. The five core needs and the questions which reveal how we believe they are being met which Koch offers are:

- † Security: whom can I trust?
- † Identity: who am I?
- † Belonging: who wants me?
- † Purpose: why am I alive?

† Competence: what do I do well?⁷

This is a way of identifying how we *believe* our core *needs* are being met. After the fall in the Garden and with the compounding effect of the impact of sin in the world, our search for answers to these questions became complicated. Other attempts have been made to define our *needs*.

Most everyone is familiar with Abraham Maslow's *Hierarchy of Needs*. His efforts provide a basic framework for a categorization of *needs* common to all humans.⁸ Maslow's hierarchy, a study in itself, provides a good reference point for our purposes.

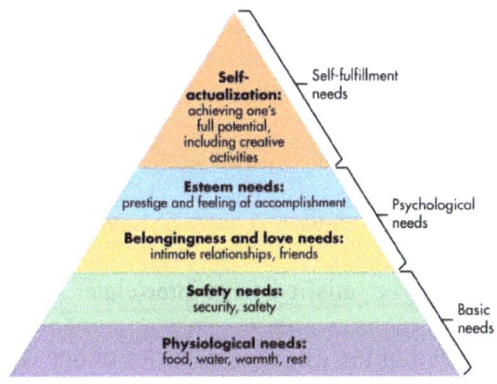

---

[7] Kathy Koch, PhD, *Five to Thrive: How to Determine if Your Core Needs are Being Met (And What to do When They're Not)*, (Chicago: Moody Publishers, 2005, 2020), 20.

[8] Saul McLeod, "Maslow's Hierachy of Needs," *SimplyPsychology* (March 20, 2020), accessed April 21, 2020. https://www.simplypsychology.org/maslow.html

We could add other terms to the list of legitimate *needs* such as acceptance, approval, growth, love, contribution, significance, variety, and perhaps many others. Unless you live in a situation where your basic *needs* as defined by Maslow are not being addressed, your list will likely fall into his categories of psychological and self-fulfillment needs.

Among other things, the fact that we all share a base set of legitimate *needs* serves as a leveling factor. It puts us on the same plane in a sense and provides a basis for connecting with others in our discussions of the spiritual heart. We are all in the same boat so to speak. Whether you are rich or poor, a white-collar professional or a blue-collar professional, a teacher or a student—it does not matter. We all have a common set of legitimate human *needs*.

All *needs* relate to a complex of *desires, beliefs, and values*—specifically *beliefs* regarding how those *needs* can be met and *desires* can be satisfied. This interrelated complex motivates and informs all of the various categories of our *behaviors*. Regardless, the core or hub of our spiritual heart consists of whatever we have *believed*. It is the root underlying all *behaviors*. This is why there are so many passages where the spiritual heart is associated with *beliefs* and *behaviors*.

What are our Beliefs?

Just as we have different categories of *needs*, our *beliefs* fall into different categories. For example, pause for a moment and consider the *beliefs* which you have embraced to be true in regard to the following.

- † God – Who is He? What does He expect of you? What is acceptable to Him? How do we satisfy Him?
- † Your identity – How do you define yourself? How do you perceive others to define you? How do you see yourself when you look into the mirror of your spiritual heart? When you engage in self-talk, inner communication? Does your past define you? How? Does your work or career define you? Have you believed what others have said about you? If you are a Christian, how does God define you? Do you accept God's definition? Only academically or have you internalized it, made it your own?
- † Your purpose – Is it to make money? Have a family? Live and die comfortably? If you are a Christian, how does your *belief* in your purpose align to God's purpose for your life?

- † Family – Do you have consciously defined beliefs about family? What is your responsibility to your family? What is your role within the family? What is the responsibility of others to you within the family? Do your beliefs align to the Bible's instruction and principles?
- † Friends – Do you have healthy, transparent relationships with a group of friends whom you can trust? Do you believe that you cannot live without friends? Do you have co-dependencies or enabling relationships you call friendships and consider that to be normal?
- † Work, employment, career—Do you *believe* work to be something forced upon you? Do you *believe* that your security and happiness is dependent upon your career? What is a biblical and truth-based view of work?
- † Parents – If you are an adult, is your life independent of your parents even though you may still love them? Do you love them? If not, do you *believe* it is possible for you to love them? What is your view of parenting? Are your *beliefs* about parenting and your role as a parent consistent with truth? Do you have a consciously constructed parenting model? Or, are you following patterns of others

without consideration of whether those patterns align with truth principles?

† Marriage, sex, intimacy, role of husband/wife – What *beliefs* have you embraced? Those of the entertainment media? Feminism? Same sex partners? The domineering husband/submissive wife model? What is the biblical model? Do you *believe* in it?

† Money, wealth, spending, saving, giving – What are your *beliefs* regarding money? Wealth accumulation? Should you spend as much as or more than you make? Is borrowing appropriate? Anytime? Under what conditions? How much should you save? Give? What is the biblical view regarding making money, accumulating wealth, spending, saving, giving? Does God disapprove of money and wealth?

† Church – What is the role of church? What does a biblical church look like?

† Sports, entertainment, exercise, leisure – What do you *believe* to be the proper role of these in your life? Is there a biblical perspective of these pursuits?

† Past or present abusive treatment from or to others – Do you have never-again policies? Do you *believe* that you can

forgive? Have you forgiven yourself by claiming God's forgiveness? Is your self-talk spiritually healthy? How has the abuse impacted your identity and the *beliefs* about yourself which you have internalized?

† What about other *belief* and *belief systems* involving such things as children, education, death, eternity, role of government and human responsibility?

The Wisdom of the World Leaves Us Thirsty

Truth and wisdom relevant to each of these *beliefs* and *belief systems* flood the pages of the Bible. The world also has a type of wisdom as well—some of which aligns with the truths of the Bible and some of which does not. When the wisdom of the world aligns with some truth found in the Bible, the wisdom of the world can deceive us so that we internalize the wisdom of the world as a substitute for the eternal truth, the thirst-quenching water of life (cf. Jn 7:38). There is always enough truth in the lie to make it deceptive (1 Cor 1:19–20). The biblically based discernment necessary to enable us to ferret truth from the lie takes time. All truth is God's truth, yet all of the principles that allow us to evaluate all truth are contained in the Bible. We float on the sea of notions until we form truth-based rudders in our spiritual hearts.

During a dinner last summer with friends who have family connections in the Middle East, we discussed the perpetual state of hostility there. My friend observed that perhaps proper education would solve the problem. Obviously, my friend believes that education is helpful. It can be a path to a better financial future instead of the poverty and lack of hope in this world for people living in areas dominated by evil ideologies and oppressive governments. But, does education provide a solution in itself? Certainly, the right education may provide more employment options and greater earnings potential which, in turn, may provide greater stability and the possibility for greater flourishing. But, does education always promote *beliefs* aligned to truth in all knowledge domains? Of course not—and my friend would agree. Education alone does not address the *needs* of the spiritual heart. Only God can do that.

Any increased living standard that results from the right educational background only addresses certain *needs*. Any "happiness" attained as a result of an education is not the same as "joy" and contentment which was possessed by such believers as

Paul who had learned to be content (2 Cor 12:10; Phil 4:11; 1 Tm 6:6, 8 cf. Heb 13:5). As Paul matured in his spiritual heart, his *beliefs* were transformed through the renewal of his mind. There was a replacement of wrong *beliefs* which had been dominant with truths related to his new identity in Christ (Phil 3:8–16; 4:11). The impact upon all of the components of his spiritual heart—his perception of his *needs* and *desires*, his *beliefs,* his *values*, his *motivations*, and all of his *behaviors* were being brought into alignment with truth. Like Paul, we are called upon to not succumb to the wisdom of the world, but to be discerning and use the truth in Scripture as our filter—a filter to sift *beliefs* and *belief systems* aligned to truth from those which are not (Phil 1:9; Heb 4:12; 5:14).

Spiritual Heart Health

The *desires* of our spiritual heart are conflicted. I have had to ask myself on many occasions just how much I desire to be conformed to the image of Jesus. Gaining an understanding of what the image of Jesus looks like is one challenge, but actually having the *desire* to be conformed to His image is another (cf. Rom 7:18; 13:14; Gal 5:17; 5:24; 2 Tm 3:12; 1 Jn 2:16).

Each of us needs to perform a spiritual heart health assessment. A spiritually unhealthy heart is a heart that has conflicted *desires* and *beliefs*. On the one hand, we *desire* to be like Him to the extent we have grasped all that He has done for us and made available for us. That *desire* grows as we grow in our internalization of His Word with the ministry of the Holy Spirit to our hearts. As the apostle Paul states in Philippians 2:13, "it is God who works in you, both to will and to work for his good pleasure."

On the other hand, we have *desires* related to our *needs* in this world—*desires* which are tightly interwoven with *beliefs* about what will bring us some happiness and pleasure and allow us to escape, even if briefly, the pressures of life. These *desires*, and the *beliefs* associated with them, create a conflict in our hearts. The transformation and renewal of our spiritual heart is integral to Paul's command to "…work out your own salvation with fear and trembling" (Phil 2:12b). "Working out our own salvation" includes adjusting our *beliefs* to align with God's perspective regarding how our *needs* can be met. How we answer questions such as the following can surface symptoms of a spiritually unhealthy heart.

† What *beliefs* and *belief systems* have I internalized (embraced as my own) regarding how I align to God's

righteousness in my life? Do I *believe* I can somehow make up to God for past sins by better performance now? Have I trusted His provision through Jesus' death for my sin so that my guilt is laid at His feet and I no longer carry that load? Do I fully trust His character? His word? The answers to these questions identify the trajectory of our spiritual hearts.

† Why is a progressive and ongoing alignment to God's righteousness in my life important to God and His *desires* for me?

† What habituated complex of *desires, beliefs, values*, and *motivations* underpin any of my *behaviors* which do not align to God's righteous standards?

† Do I have addictions (substance abuse, spending patterns, debt, pornography) which I can associate with unmet *needs* or *desires* for approval, acceptance, or distorted identity?

† Do I have *beliefs* that produce unrealistic *expectations* of others? Myself? God?

† Do I have insecurities, fears, phobias, anxieties, or inferiority complexes which in turn affect my *relationships*?

The **_beliefs_** that we have **internalized** through conscious choice or through unconscious influences (other people, culture, media messaging, etc.) regarding how our **_needs_** can be met are the **central-most component** of the spiritual heart and the **central-most issue** in our spiritual walk as believers in the all-sufficient work of Jesus our Lord (e.g. Rom 12:2; Eph 4:17–31).

Questions for Consideration:
- † How would you define your core needs?
- † Do the questions posed by Dr. Kathy Koch provide help you relate core needs to beliefs you have regarding how the needs can be met?
- † How do you define your identity? How would others define you? Is your definition of identity aligned with your identity in Christ? Does God define you in the same way you define yourself?

Chapter 4 – Behaviors: Portals of Insight into Flourishing or Failing

The phrase "spiritual heart" embraces the immaterial and material nature of humans. It is the repository of the *beliefs* and *values* which inform one's *expectations*, *emotions*, and observable *behaviors*. It represents the combined function of soul (eternal nature) and body (temporal nature).

Behaviors of Israel—Portals into the Mixed Beliefs of a Religious Society and Culture

The *belief system* of the Jewish people of Roman occupied Israel in the 1st Century A.D. included an *expectation* of a Messiah who would deliver Israel from her Gentile oppressors and establish a kingdom with its capital at Jerusalem. There was basis for that *expectation* in the Scriptures (e.g. 2 Sa 7:9–29). Yet, with wonderful exceptions (e.g. Zecharias, Elizabeth, Mary, Simeon, Anna, and others "waiting for the redemption of Jerusalem"—Lk 2:38), most of Israel had lost their understanding and *belief* in God's purpose for them—to be a light to the Gentiles. God's purpose for them was to be His obedient agent through which He would draw the Gentiles to the one God, Israel's God (Ge 26:4; Dt 28:1, 12; 1 Chr 16:24, 31; Ps 9:11; 22:27; 57:9; 67:1–7; 87:1–7; 98:2–3; 105:1; 117:1; Is 2:2; 51:4–5; 52:15; 56; 66:18–21; Mi 4:2; Hg 2:7; Zec 2:11; Mal 3:12).

Instead, they *desired* all the blessings God promised to them as Abraham's descendants (Gen 12:1–3, 7; 13:14–17; 15:1–21; 17:1–14; 22:15–18; 26:2–4; 28:13–14; 35:11–12), but instead of drawing the Gentiles to the one true God, they followed after the false gods of the Gentiles. Instead of demonstrating their faith (*belief*) through obedient *behaviors* consistent with His instructions to them, they pursued a path independent of God. Their *desire* for security and acceptance became attached to *beliefs* that denied the goodness and character of their God. Their *behaviors* became a reflection of their anthropocentric focus upon their own glorification—not the God who loved them and called them for a special purpose. They lost their identity.

Later in their history, self-righteousness based upon law observance and racial heritage dominated their identity with a sense of entitlement—especially the religious leadership. Jesus, the very embodiment of truth, did not fit their *belief system* and *expectations* of the Messiah.

The untruth (or lie) on the other side of a half-truth leavens the whole (Mt 13:33; 16:6, 11–12; 1 Cor 5:6–8; Gal 5:9). What they *believed* to be true was based upon half-truths. The *behaviors* emerging from the half-truths that they accepted as truth led to Jesus' death on a Cross. They illustrated the principle that when our *belief systems* consist of a stew-like mixture of misinterpreted and misapplied Scripture passages combined with anthropocentric *desires* and *expectations*, we remain afloat on a sea of false notions with damaging consequences to ourselves and others in the raging storms of life. First Century A.D. Israel reflected this principle in their *behaviors* collectively and as individuals. Their *beliefs* and *belief systems* consisted of a mixture of misappropriated and misunderstood truths of Scripture related to the Messiah—a dangerous combination of half-truths.

The New Believers of Corinth – The Disadvantage of Beliefs and Behavioral Baggage

Later in the First Century A.D., a culturally advanced people existed who had a heritage of great thinkers such as Plato who argued against the weaknesses of democracy; Aristotle who promoted views such as natural rights, republican government, and the rule of law; and Epicurus who promoted ideas of human flourishing.

In time, that people became impressed by their wisdom and their culture was consumed with the pursuit of wisdom, idolatry, and athletic events. They were blind to their true status of moral decay and their trajectory as a people. They considered themselves too advanced to give serious consideration to a God promoted by a tribal people.

After all, they had their own gods of their mythology who had come in the flesh. Enter Paul—the most significant change agent in human history other than Jesus Christ. Many came to *believe* under Paul's ministry in particular—in addition to others who came to *believe* under the ministries of other men such as Apollos and Peter. Yet, they entered the Christian faith and life with the baggage of prior practices and *behaviors* that needed to be brought into alignment with their new identity in Christ—not their culture. Their culture would pass as do all things of this world.

The new Christ-followers of Corinth were at a disadvantage. Their cultural marketplace was saturated with pagan religions, anthropocentric philosophies, and idolatrous practices. This culture had been absorbed for years into the *beliefs* and life practices of all Corinthians. Continued transformation was needed in the new believers even after their acceptance of Jesus. *Beliefs* about all spheres of life needed to be adjusted to align with truth from God.

What We Believe to be True Is the Basis for Our Behaviors

When we come to faith in Jesus, we have an eternal destiny secured for us by the work of Jesus. However, between that point of faith in Jesus' work for us and our death, we are called to undergo a transformation of all of our *beliefs* and become conformed to His image (Rom 12:2 cf. 8:29). God desires that our spiritual hearts—the entirety of our being, our *beliefs, values, expectations, emotions,* and *behaviors*—be brought into alignment with His heart. Like the new believers in Corinth, we carry baggage of old *beliefs* and *behaviors* into our new lives in Christ. In fact, even after we believe in Jesus' all-sufficient work and God imputes to us His righteousness, we are still quite capable in our fallen state and world of accepting wrong *beliefs* to be true. To the extent we have accepted wrong *beliefs* to be true is the extent to which we've yet to have our spiritual hearts transformed through the renewal of our minds.

Today, believers are at different points in this process of transformation and conformity. Some are in the proverbial ditch due to false *beliefs* they have accepted to be true—even some which are sourced from pulpits, academia, and society at large. To one extent or another, we've all been there and perhaps we are there currently to one degree or another. Like us, the new believers of Corinth needed truth in order to have a chance to identify and make a decision about replacing wrong *beliefs* with new *beliefs*. Otherwise, their *behaviors* and identities would not be associated with Jesus but with their past. Their *behaviors* were the portal into the old *beliefs* which they carried like ugly baggage into their new royal status as children and ambassadors for the King. In chapter after chapter of his letters to them, Paul peers through the portal to address the change needed.

We have all heard the statement, "perception is reality." Well, the *beliefs* we accept to be true are truth to us regardless of whether they align to the actual truth or not. The subjective relativism of our day produces statements to the effect of "that is your truth" or "his truth" or "her truth." Whatever we *believe* to be true becomes the basis for our *behaviors* (Rom 1:25 cf. 1 Cor 13:6; 2 Thes 2:12).

Behaviors provide windows or portals into our spiritual hearts. We observe the *beliefs* of people in action through the portals provided by *behaviors* such as their *verbal patterns*, *relational patterns*, and their *pursuits and priorities*. We observe <u>overt</u> *behaviors* in others and in ourselves. We can observe <u>internal</u> *behaviors* in ourselves—internal *behaviors* such as *self-talk*, *rationales*, *justifications*, and *expectations*. To do so requires that we hit the pause button on the busyness of our lives, mentally step outside of ourselves, and examine our lives as if we were viewing ourselves through another set of eyes. When we do so objectively and without the internal rationalization and justification that so often obscures our view, we tend to see our *behavioral patterns* differently. The *behaviors* we observe are the tip of an iceberg. The causes of those *behaviors* are rooted in *beliefs*.

Throughout our lives, we learn to adjust our *behaviors* based upon our *beliefs* regarding their success or non-success in meeting our *needs* and fulfilling our *desires*. In time, *behaviors* that seem to satisfy to some degree our *beliefs* and *expectations* become habituated as we practice what we deem successful over and over again. They become our own. They are internalized. They become a part of our identity—how we define ourselves.

Our lives, like an airplane on semi-autopilot, consist of mostly unconscious reactions to the events and relationships in our daily lives. For the most part, we do not give conscious thought to our habituated relationship *behavior patterns*. That is ok when they are healthy and aligned with truth principles. However, to the extent that our *belief system* and *behavior complex* is misaligned with truth, the adverse effects of the Fall will be acute. God uses the inevitable pain of unmet *expectations* and destructive *behaviors* rooted in *beliefs* misaligned to truth. The pain should alert us to the compromised health of our spiritual hearts. Hopefully, the pain causes us to recognize our need for truth and our dependence upon Him. The fallen nature desires independence, autonomy, self-glorification—effectively self-deification. This was illustrated most vividly in the father of lies—Satan (Jn 8:44 cf. Is 14:12–14; Ez 28:11b–19).

Anthropocentric Beliefs Lead to Self-Deification and Misplaced Identity

As believers in Jesus, we aspire to (or should aspire to) the objective of conformity to the image of Christ (Rom 8:29). We also have the option of conformity to the world's *values, priorities, relational patterns and strategies,* and *verbal patterns.* We can *rationalize* and *justify* behaviors based upon the world's constant message that "you deserve it" or "you are entitled to it." These messages align to the *priorities* of the fallen nature. They align to much of the world. They are built upon the *belief* that the most important objective is to maximize pleasure and minimize pain. After all, we are the center of our world as creatures independent of God. The person who *believes* he or she is independent from God has effectively become his or her own god—"like God" (Ge 3:5 cf. Ez 28:2).

The god of the West (and much of the rest of the world) is not the God of Scripture. This false god is the god of "moralistic therapeutic deism" (MTD).[9] He (or she) is the paternalistic (or

---

[9] This phrase is mentioned in numerous books and publications. One example is Christian Smith and Melinda Lundquist Denton, *Soul Searching* (Oxford: Oxford University Press, 2005), 162–70 as cited in John S. Dickerson,

maternalistic), loving grandparent figure who is happy with everyone who is moral. This MTD god exists to make you happy too.[10] This is a drastically different god than the Son of God, Jesus Christ, to Whose image we are to be conformed (Rom 8:29) through the renewal of our minds (Rom 12:2). The *belief system* and *behavior patterns* built upon the MTD god foundation are different from, even opposed to, the God of Scripture. Accordingly, the sacrificial life of Jesus and the first century apostles and Christ-followers contrasts starkly with much of the church today. Why? What is reason for the difference? Our fallen, natural-self internalized *belief* and *behavior system patterns* individually and collectively are ultimately anthropocentric and rooted in a desire for self-glorification.

To the extent that our *beliefs* misalign with truth, the result is a divided spiritual heart, suffering, broken or unhealthy

---

The Great Evangelical Recession (Grand Rapids, Michigan: Baker Books, 2013), 105.

[10] The basic tenets of MTD that I have been able to distill are: 1) a deity created the world and watches over it; 2) this deity desires harmony—a view consistent with most of the world's major religions; 3) the large concern of this god is human happiness and self-worth; 4) this god is approached when problems exist; otherwise, it is comforting to know god is there; and 5) good people go to be with this god when they die.

relationships, wounded spiritual hearts, addictions, and, in many cases, adverse impacts upon the body. In his epistle, James calls the divided spiritual heart "doubleminded" (Jas 1:8; 4:8). The divided spiritual heart or the "doubleminded" person has conflicting *beliefs, rationales, justifications,* and *expectations*. When we have a divided spiritual heart, we waiver between *beliefs* aligned with the truth and *beliefs* misaligned with the truth (cf. 1 Jn 1:6).[11]

The Path to Spiritual Heart Renewal

As I have practiced the framework or model described in this book, I discovered that the path of spiritual heart renewal and restoration consists of several key interrelated steps. The omission or episodic practice of these steps results in a perpetual spiritual childhood or adolescence at best. These steps interrelate and overlap with each other. They do not occur in a chronological sequence of one through five, nor do we complete any particular step 100 percent before the next step begins. In fact, like the fundamentals of

---

[11] Readers wishing to explore the subject of a divided spiritual heart may want to consider Steve Fair, *Journey into the Divided Heart – Facing the Defense Mechanisms That Hinder True Emotional Healing* (Oviedo, Florida: Higher Life Publishing, 2020).

a golf swing, our misapplication of the steps leads only to poor outcomes regardless of how long you or I have been on the golf course of life. Spiritual momentum demands the continual and consistent practice of the following steps.

† Identify false *beliefs* through objective evaluation by stepping outside of oneself.
† *Desire* to be conformed and transformed.
† Repentance (change of *belief*, thinking) regarding false *beliefs*.
† Internalization of the truth (making truth one's own) into the spiritual heart with conscious intent.
† Submission or yielding to truth in daily circumstances—testings, pressures, and exigencies of life.

If we are waiting for a feeling or some external stimuli to accomplish something supernatural or transforming so that we are propelled forward by some mystical force, we will be approaching the final chapters of our life still wondering when and if this magical moment will arrive. We will always consider that day as something future. If you have not yet placed your trust in Jesus, please do not wait for some future epiphany or for some Nirvana set of conditions to exist when you have other life goals accomplished.

The apostle Paul states that "...*behold, now is the favorable time: behold, now is the day of salvation*" (2 Cor 6:2 ESV).

Applying these steps consistently requires conscious intent. They do not happen by default nor do they occur naturally in our lives. Our sinful nature resists and opposes the changes which occurs with the application of these steps. The resistance to change arises from the conflict with our existing *desires*; the false *beliefs* and complex of *expectations* and *rationales* we have built; our perceived "success" with our *relational strategies*; the *beliefs* which others have accepted to be true when they conflict with the truth of Scripture; and by the conscious changes to *behaviors* which is needed to align to truth principles.

Where There is Change, There is Pain

There will be pain associated with change. Our worldly identity must yield to our identity in Christ. While we seek to engage in a loving and Christlike way with others as we mature in our walk of heart transformation, the circle of those whose spiritual hearts beat in harmony becomes smaller. Any superficialities in our activities and relationships become more apparent. We will examine these steps in chapter 8 in more detail.

The category of *behaviors* I've entitled *"relational patterns and strategies"* provides us with insight into *beliefs* and *expectations* we have accepted as truth which are not based upon truth. When we discuss the problems we experience in relationships with people at work, in families, in social situations, and in marriages, inevitably, the problems can be traced to the *beliefs*, *desires* and *expectations* connected to the real and perceived *needs* of all of the parties involved. The husband and wife who are finding their marriage to have drifted into more of a shared living arrangement with little to no intimacy can begin the path to a restored and renewed relationship when they identify the gap between their *belief systems* and how their respective *belief system*s are informing their *behaviors*. Most of the time, this requires the help of a trained counselor or pastor. It is normal to need assistance with the objectivity necessary to step outside of ourselves—especially at first.

As we navigate through life in a spiritually fallen state in a spiritually fallen world, life forces us to develop *patterns of relating* to others in an attempt to have our *needs* met and *desires* fulfilled.

Inevitably, no one begins this journey equipped with all necessary and relevant biblical truths. At best, the journey begins with loving parents in a stable home setting where some truths consistent with biblical instruction are taught and learned. While beneficial, even the more idyllic home setting may not address all of the wrong *beliefs* and *belief systems* to which people are exposed in academia and the world at large. Many of these wrong *beliefs* and *belief systems* are unconsciously absorbed into the spiritual heart—even by believers. These wrong *beliefs* and *belief systems* which are at the root of destructive and spiritually unhealthy behaviors become the source of brokenness and/or failed spiritual potential to greater or lesser degrees. This is the great spiritual war not fought with earthly weapons and implements—the war to which the apostle Paul referred in Ephesians 6:10–18. We are on the battlefield of that war until the day we die. None of us exit the spiritual battlefield without having suffered its devastation to one degree or another. None pass through this life unscathed.

Behavior-Based Portal Examples

The idyllic Christian home hasn't existed since the Garden of Eden prior to the fall. Most of us come from at least some degree of a dysfunctional parenting and family setting. These environments impact the *belief systems* we accept and internalize in incredible ways—ways that establish the trajectory of our lives and the relationships we have throughout our lives.

Examples of *relational patterns* emerging from the spiritual heart of a believer in Jesus Christ who has experienced renewal and restoration will be mentioned in chapter 8. However, it may be helpful to look at some examples of *relational patterns* and *strategies* that are portals into a spiritual heart that may or may not be so healthy. I doubt that a comprehensive list exists, so I do not propose a list that covers all possibilities. Terminology and definitions vary somewhat.

Each of us have had episodic occurrences of at least some of these relational mechanisms in our lives. However, we are looking for the more pernicious patterns which reveal a pervasive *belief system* within the spiritual heart. The *behavior* is the tip of the iceberg of an underlying *belief system* within the spiritual heart.

Belief systems not rooted in the truth produce problematic *behavior patterns*. Below the surface of the tip of the iceberg (i.e. the *behaviors* we observe) lies an interlaced web of *beliefs, expectations, rationales* and *justifications*—all built upon either truth or an untruth, a lie, until the transformation of the heart occurs.

I have found the following list of *behaviors* to be helpful as a starting point.[12] The examples of each *behavior* are purposefully simplistic to illustrate the specific *behavior*. In reality, our *behaviors* are most often an interrelated complex. Nevertheless, this list includes defense mechanisms we employ in order to avoid pain or maximize perceived pleasure when we are anthropocentric in focus versus Christ-centric in focus. As you read through the list, you may ask yourself—"how would a Christ-follower engage in this behavior in a Christ-honoring way?" If that question cannot be answered, then you might want to ask—"what is a Christ-honoring

---

[12] John M. Grohol, Psy.D., "15 Common Defense Mechanisms," *PsychCentral* (June 3, 2019), accessed April 21, 2020. https://psychcentral.com/lib/15-common-defense-mechanisms/ . See also Kendra Cherry, "20 Common Defense Mechanisms Used for Anxiety," *VeryWellMind* (January 22, 2020), accessed May 2, 2020.
https://www.verywellmind.com/defense-mechanisms-2795960 and Saul McLeod, "Defense Mechanisms," *Simply Psychology* (2019), accessed May 2, 2020. https://www.simplypsychology.org/defense-mechanisms.html .

counterpart to this behavior? What beliefs would support a Christ-honoring behavior?"

† *Denial* – the refusal to accept reality or fact as if a painful event, thought or feeling did not exist. *Example*: Joe, a functioning alcoholic denies the existence of a drinking problem and combines that denial with *rationalization* and *justification* of the *behavior*. Joe argues that he is functioning well in his job and relationships. *Example*: Cindy has racked up a half of a year's salary in credit card debt within the past year and refuses to acknowledge the looming debt crisis she faces if this pattern continues. *Example*: Bill's son John bullied several other children at school. The school administration contacted Bill about John's *behavior*. Bill immediately denies the possibility that his son who adores his dad could behave this way. In fact, Bill states that the other children need to grow some spine.

† *Regression* – the reversion to an earlier stage of development in the face of unacceptable thoughts or impulses. *Example*: Sally cannot land a job. Stress engulfed her life as financial pressures mounted associated with the layoff a year ago. She finds that leaving bed is becoming

increasingly difficult. She rises later and later on a daily basis. Her bed has become a protective womb sheltering her from facing reality and engaging in normal, daily activities. *Example*: Fear, anger and growing sexual impulses overwhelms Tim, an adolescent, as he attempts to embrace the challenges of identity in a toxic, public, inner-city school environment. Tim clings to his parents while at the same time remaining somewhat isolated from his schoolmates.

† *Acting out* – performing an extreme behavior in order to express thoughts or feelings the person feels incapable of otherwise expressing. *Example*: Carl owns and manages a successful company with 500 well paid employees. He founded the company, pays top dollar for his employees, and is well respected for his business knowledge and philanthropic endeavors. Yet, when Carl wants quick results, he displays anger in physical ways like pounding the desk.

† *Dissociation* – occurs when a person loses track of time and/or person and instead, finds another representation of themselves in order to continue in the moment. People who

have a history of any kind of childhood abuse often suffer from some form of dissociation. In extreme cases, dissociation can lead a person to believe that they have multiple selves. A person who dissociates can disconnect from the real world for a time and live in a different world that is not cluttered with thoughts, feelings or memories that are otherwise unbearable. *Example*: Gary has a well-paying job as a senior manager with a manufacturing concern. However, Gary *believes* that he would have gained the respect of his father, Kelly, who is a war hero, had he gone into the Marines and become a fighter pilot. Gary desperately *desires* to hear his father tell him how proud he is of Gary. Gary frequently disconnects from his surroundings during lunch and at other times during the day as he imagines himself being awarded heroic actions in a military conflict.

† *Compartmentalization* – a lesser form of dissociation in which parts of oneself are separated from awareness of other parts and behaving as if one had separate sets of values. *Example*: Carolyn, who leads women's Bible studies at First United Methodist Church and runs a

successful craft business, earns about $25,000 a year in selling used books from a spare room next to a garage on her property. Carolyn considers some of those cash-basis sales to be non-business related because they benefit poorer families with children who would not have access to the books otherwise. She does not report those cash-basis sales (at an additional discount) to be taxable income since her margin is so reduced. If asked directly if she *believes* that cheating on one's tax return is wrong, she would say "yes." However, since she has compartmentalized her cash-basis sales, she does not consider the non-reporting of otherwise taxable income to be wrong. Two disparate *value* and *behavior systems* compete in Carolyn's life.

† *Projection* – the misattribution of a person's undesired thoughts, feelings, or impulses onto another person who does not have those thoughts, feelings, or impulses.

Example: When Eric gets angry at Rebecca, he accuses her of not listening. In fact, Eric is not listening and his failure to listen actually leads to misunderstanding which leads to his anger.

- *Repression* – the unconscious blocking of unacceptable thoughts, feelings and impulses. Since it is a largely unconscious behavior and relational pattern, people have little control over its occurrence. Repressed memories generally surface later when triggered by certain events. *Example*: The examples are too numerous of people who in their childhood experienced verbal, physical or sexual abuse from an adult whom they trusted. The repressed memory of that experience surfaces later when a trigger event occurs. Examples of trigger events could include a boss or spouse who becomes angry and yells or a scene appears in a movie of a person being abused.
- *Displacement* – the redirecting of thoughts, feelings and impulses otherwise directed toward one person or object but expressed toward another person or object. People often use displacement when they cannot express their feelings in a safe manner to the person who is the object of those feelings. *Example*: Josh gets angry at his boss at work but does not express anger there for fear of being fired. However, when Josh comes home from work, he releases his pent-up anger and expresses it toward Jane, his spouse,

over the most insignificant misplacement of the newspaper. Josh kicks the dog while looking for the misplaced item.

† *Intellectualization* – the overemphasis on thought to the virtual exclusion of emotions when confronted with an unacceptable impulse, situation or behavior. Otherwise, the emotions would help to mediate and place the thoughts into a more natural, human context. Intellectualization creates distance from the impulse, event or behavior. *Example:* Pancreatic cancer attacks Kathy's body. Kathy directs her thirty-year interest in natural foods and herbal treatments for various ailments to a solution for cancer, the focus of all of her intellectual energies. She never discusses nor plans for the possibility that the cancer will metastasize.

† *Rationalization* – placing something in a different light or offering a different explanation for one's *perceptions* or *behaviors* in the face of a changing reality. *Rationalization* and *justification* are essentially two sides of the same coin. *Rationalization* leads to *justification*. *Example*: Jack *rationalizes* that his golf outing this Saturday is vital to securing a deal with a new client, thus securing his place in the firm. His *justification*—he is the income provider while

his wife Beth takes care of the kids and the home. In the meantime, Jack pushed the golf outing to occur this Saturday to minimize the time he had to be home with Beth's parents in town. Jack *rationalizes* his decision with seemingly valid *justification*, yet Jack's *rationalization* is not aligned with his true *motives*.

† *Undoing* – the attempt to take back an unconscious *behavior* or thought that is unacceptable or hurtful. By undoing, we attempt to counteract the damage done by a previous action with the *desire* and *expectation* that the two will balance each other. *Example:* Tom commented that the dinner which Liz spent the afternoon preparing was "not the best" without realizing how much time Liz had spent preparing it. Tom attempts to recover by praising Liz on how wonderful her newest hairstyle looks. Tom probably has a lot of undoing in order to dig out of his hole.

† *Sublimation* – the channeling of unacceptable impulses, thoughts and emotions into more acceptable ones. Sublimation can be practiced with humor or fantasy and can be a legitimate and helpful *relational pattern* or defense mechanism in some cases. The question we must ask in

order to determine the difference—what *belief system* aligns with the *behavior*? Humor, when used as a *relational pattern* or defense mechanism, can channel unacceptable impulses or thoughts into a light-hearted story or joke. Humor reduces the intensity of a situation and places a cushion of laughter between the person and the situation. Fantasy is the channeling of unacceptable or unattainable desires into imagination. *Example:* Hal suspended his pursuit of a master's degree so he could care for his father who contracted cancer. Hal channels the negative impulses and thoughts about the suspension of his educational objectives into looking at the situation differently. Hal focuses upon what he can learn in the process of caring for his father. Hal translates the experience into becoming a better Christian leader in business, improved home life, and sharing truth that he will learn through the process with others facing similar circumstances. *Example:* Jake is in his late twenties and has four years of Big Four M&A consulting plus his masters behind him. He is still single and is channeling his sexual drive into an obsessive focus upon rigorous exercise, mountain climbing, biking, and hiking and is considering adding training for a triathlon over the next few months.

† *Compensation* – a process of psychologically counterbalancing perceived weaknesses by emphasizing strength in other areas. By emphasizing and focusing upon one's strengths, a person is attempting to counter-balance their weaknesses with their strengths. Compensation can also be a legitimate practice. It depends upon the underlying *belief system* and *motivation* for the practice of it. *Example:* Sam says "I may not know how to cook, but I can sure do the dishes." This illustrates an innocuous use of compensation. *Example:* Sue believes if she only had a more perfect figure, she would have more self-confidence and garner more interest from the opposite sex, so Sue undergoes augmentation surgery to enhance her breast size to a DD from her current C. Sue is probably using compensation as a relational strategy in a way that does not reflect a *belief system* aligned with truth principles. Her *relational strategy* may be aligned to a lie Sue has believed about herself.

† *Assertiveness* – the emphasis of a person's needs or thoughts in a manner that is respectful, direct and firm. Assertiveness can be good or bad depending upon the underlying *belief system* and *motives*. When the motivation stems from a *belief system* in which controlling our circumstances and the people with whom we interact is central, then we should question whether the *behavior* aligns to truth-based *beliefs*. *Example:* Pat is assertive, but polite in board meetings as the only female on the board of directors. She has won the respect of all of the board and senior leadership in the company because she balances assertiveness with a polite and respectful tone with everyone with whom she interacts. Pat's *behavior pattern* is based upon a *belief system* that balances biblical truth with the realities of the corporate world. She *desires* to glorify Christ in her life while demonstrating Christlikeness in all she does. *Example:* Jack constantly and consistently asserts his position as board chairman and CEO driven by a *motive* and *belief system* that micro-management and control of people achieves results. Jack's relations strategy fails due to misalignment with truth-based leadership principles.

† *Enablement* – the most often unconscious (or possibly conscious) facilitation of another's immature, wrong, or even destructive *behavior patterns* (sometimes addictions) through ignoring, compensating, excusing, covering up, aiding in the *rationalization/justification*, concealing, and/or continuing to provide financial/logistical support.[13] There is a fine line between enablement and helping someone to work through an issue in their life. Often the enabler and the person involved in the immature, wrong or destructive behavior pattern are codependent. The enabler depends upon the other individual for financial, emotional or some other need and the one enabled, depends upon the enabler to continue in some type of habituated *behavior*. Enablement and being enabled are *relational strategies* built in part upon a system of *beliefs, rationalizations, justifications*, and *expectations* that our *desires* and *needs* can only be met via another fallen individual. We develop such coping strategies in an attempt to control or manage our life situations with a goal of minimizing pain and maximizing

---

[13] The definition and description I offer here of enablement is my own and is not included in any of the previous sources cited.

pleasure. The question we should ask if we find ourselves in such a *relational pattern* should be whether this emulates any behaviors Jesus demonstrated or endorsed and if not, what *mental* and *behavioral patterns* would reflect the character of God and Jesus? *Example*: The addict is generally characterized by *behaviors* designed to manipulate and control. Instead of confronting Zack about his drinking, Peggy *believes* that conflict and strife under any circumstance indicates a personal misalignment with God. Avoid conflict at all cost. Zack senses Peggy's penchant for peace over confrontation. Peggy continues to maintain all other aspects of the marriage and home life as normal as possible while also insuring that Zack's increased drinking falls into the category of "social drinking" in all conversations. Peggy enables Zack's wrong behavior.

This list of examples of relational *behaviors* represent a sample of the universe of *behavior* possibilities. If we peer carefully through the behavioral portal, we will locate the *beliefs, values, motivations,* and *expectations* which underlie our *behaviors*—as well as the *needs* and *desires* we are trying to meet. The identification of that interconnection is critical to assessing the health of our spiritual hearts.

Hopefully, this chapter conveys the vital or symbiotic relationship within our spiritual hearts between our *needs*, *desires*, *beliefs*, *values*, *motives*, and *behaviors*. This highly interconnected and complex set of components of the spiritual heart requires renewal, restoration, and transformation. To use my earlier analogy, this complex of components compares to the rubber band ball that represents the spiritual heart. It makes the isolated analysis of any component of the spiritual heart similar to an attempt to extract a single rubber band. The components are truly interconnected and that interconnected mass is who we are. This is why God prizes our spiritual hearts. He desires that we be drawn to His own heart so that He may fellowship with us and us with Him—just as He did with Adam and Eve in the Garden prior to the Fall.

Questions for Consideration:

† What behaviors have you adjusted due to a change of a belief? Was it the result of a belief that you changed that aligned with some truth you learned?

- Can you think of any half-truths you have accepted as complete truths which have been the basis for problematic behaviors?
- Can you identify an habituated behavioral pattern in your life and the belief and needs to which it relates?

Chapter 5 – Strongholds: The Fortification of Worst Practices

The phrase "spiritual heart" embraces the immaterial and material nature of humans. It is the repository of the *beliefs* and *values* which inform one's *expectations*, *emotions*, and observable *behaviors*. It represents the combined function of soul (eternal nature) and body (temporal nature).

What happens when we reinforce our *beliefs* by repeating the same *behaviors* over and over again? At least two things happen. First, we adjust our *belief systems* and/or manipulate our *behaviors* in the hope of achieving the outcomes or *expectations* we desire—our success criteria. Second, we habituate our practice of *behaviors* which meet our definition of success. Habituation reinforces existing *belief systems*.

Strongholds of the Spiritual Heart in Corinth

The apostle Paul recognized this concept as he ministered to the Gentile believers in Corinth. As we noted in the previous chapter, these new believers possessed *belief systems* influenced and shaped by their culture, a culture similar in many ways to our culture today. When the Gentiles in Corinth came to faith in Jesus under Paul's ministry and began to grow further under Apollos and perhaps even Peter (1 Cor 3:5–6, 10, 22), they did not undergo a frontal lobotomy and lose all of the *belief systems* from their past. Paul fills his letters to the church in Corinth with instruction in one issue after another—discord over cliques (1 Cor 3:12–20); sexual immorality within the church (1 Cor 5; 2 Cor 2:5–11); lawsuits between believers (1 Cor 6:1–11); conflicts over dietary practices (1 Cor 8); idolatry (1 Cor 10); the pursuit of certain spiritual gifts due to wrong motives (1 Cor 14); and the threat of false apostles (2 Cor 11)—not to mention instruction in a number of doctrinal truths and principles. Today, when a person comes to faith in the all-sufficient work of Christ, just like the Corinthians, transformation, renewal and restoration of **all** *belief systems* and *behaviors* takes time. Paul confronted the incorrect *beliefs* and *behaviors* of the Corinthians in chapter after chapter of his letters to them.

     Paul had a term for the complex of habituated *belief systems* and *behaviors* that he observed amongst the believers in Corinth. He called them "strongholds."

¹ I, Paul, myself entreat you, by the meekness and gentleness of Christ—I who am humble when face to face with you, but bold toward you when I am away!— ² I beg of you that when I am present I may not have to show boldness with such confidence as I count on showing against some who suspect us of walking according to the flesh. ³ For though we walk in the flesh, we are not waging war according to the flesh. ⁴ For the weapons of our warfare are not of the flesh but have divine power to destroy **strongholds**. ⁵ We destroy arguments and every lofty opinion raised against the knowledge of God, and take every thought captive to obey Christ, ⁶ being ready to punish every disobedience, when your obedience is complete. (2 Cor 10:1–6 ESV)

The Greek word translated "strongholds" (Gr. ὀχύρωμα – *ochuroma*) only occurs in this passage in the New Testament. It is

"…used figuratively of the strength of false arguments."[14] The "false arguments" or "strongholds" of the Corinthians refers to the *belief system/behavior complex* these relatively new believers carried forward like old baggage into their Christian lives—*belief systems/behavior complexes* at odds with Christlike character.

Strongholds, like concrete strengthened with rebar, form with habituated *belief systems* interconnected and reinforced by *internal* and *overt behaviors*. Strongholds are surrendered reluctantly. Strongholds are guarded and protected.

The person who attempts to guard, protect and defend spiritual strongholds does so for various reasons. Perhaps the *beliefs* which are the foundation for the stronghold have been embraced as truth so that there is blindness to the actual truth which would expose the *belief* built upon a falsehood. Perhaps an identity is fortressed in the stronghold. Perhaps the stronghold is related to a *belief* that seems to satisfy the *need* for security. Perhaps there has been a certain degree of "success" in the world using the *belief system* not aligned to truth.

---

[14] Johannes P. Louw and Eugene Albert Nida, *Greek-English Lexicon of the New Testament: Based on Semantic Domains* (New York: United Bible Societies, 1996), 83.

"Arguments and Every Lofty Opinion Raised Against the Knowledge of God"

As he opens chapter 10, Paul found it necessary to establish his authority as an apostle in view of some criticisms leveled against him—charges of cowardice, weakness, and an overextension of his authority. Paul's critics had projected their own *motives*, *beliefs* and *behaviors* onto Paul. Some, like those Paul addressed in Galatians, had twisted Paul's teaching to imply that Paul was teaching something untrue (cf. Gal 2:16–17, 20; 5:16–26). Paul uses the warfare language of a stronghold because he and his readers (and us by extension) are engaged in a spiritual war—not of the flesh and not with material implements, but a war of *beliefs*, *values*, *belief systems*, and resultant *behaviors*. Paul expresses his intention to destroy the strongholds in this spiritual war.

Paul associated strongholds with "...*arguments and every lofty opinion raised against the knowledge of God*..." (2 Cor 10:5 ESV). In this statement, Paul calls out the *rationalization and justification behavior* that is interrelated with habituated practices and *beliefs*. It is as if Paul has applied a microscope to the spiritual heart and identified the very reason for spiritual blindness. Spiritual blindness results from the hardening of the spiritual heart when we form "arguments" and "lofty opinions" contrary to the righteous standard of God's truth in order to *rationalize* and *justify* our behaviors. Like the believers of Corinth, we can develop stronghold fortresses in our spiritual hearts through the habituation of *beliefs* and *behaviors* which we harden through *rationalization* and *justification*. The Corinthians spiritual hearts were fortressed in *belief system complexes* not aligned to truth which, in many cases no doubt, had been unconsciously absorbed from their culture.

The Destruction of Strongholds – How?

So, how do we deal with strongholds in our lives? We identify and subject the *beliefs* we hold to the scrutiny of the truths and truth principles in the Bible. As we discussed in chapter 4, we use our *behaviors* as portals into the *beliefs* which underlie those *behaviors*. This pursuit is a life-long journey and it helps to team with mature believers who can be trusted to interact, share experiences, and be encouraged. The number of "one another" passages in Scripture astounds me (e.g. Rom 12:10, 16; 15:5, 7, 14;

16:16; 1 Cor 11:33; 12:25; 16:20; 2 Cor 13:11–12; Gal 5:13, 15, 26; 6:2; Eph 4:2, 32; 5:19, 21; Col 3:9, 13, 16; 1 Thes 3:12; 4:9, 18; 5:11, 15; Heb 3:13; 10:24–25; Jas 5:16; 1 Pt 1:22; 4:8–10; 5:5, 14; 1 Jn 1:7, 3:11, 23; 4:7, 11–12; 2 Jn 1:5). There are no Rambo's or one-man action heroes in the church. As much as we enjoy those characters of fantasy, a supporting cast of incredible believers surrounded the apostle Paul, a man with no equal in today's action-hero movie genres.

The believer must *desire* to be conformed and transformed if the spiritual heart is to be renewed and restored. You may say, "I don't have a desire." Paul spoke to this also when he wrote "*…for it is God who works in you, both to will and to work for his good pleasure*" (Phil 2:13 ESV). Begin the process with submission and yielding to known truth and God will work through that process to help you with *desire*. Be willing to repent or change your *beliefs*. This is the essence of true, biblical humility. Meditate on the truth of Scripture and contrast the *beliefs* and *behavior patterns* you currently hold with what they look like when aligned to the truth. This requires stepping outside yourself and examining your life objectively. It helps to have either a trained Christian counselor or pastor trained in Christian counseling. All of us have unconscious bias and trained eyes can help us see things we may not see otherwise. Finally, there must be an internalization of the truth into the spiritual heart whereby *beliefs* which do not align to the truth of Scripture are rejected, replaced, and reinforced through a repeated process of yielding. By doing so, they become our own and become a part of our new identity in Christ.

Your spiritual heart is of immense value to God. He treasures it. You should too—your heart and the hearts of others as well.

Questions for Consideration:
- † What strongholds are prevalent in the lives of people with whom you associate? In your own life?
- † Are there certain beliefs or behaviors which you have rationalized and justified in spite of becoming aware of truth which would otherwise refute them?
- † Are there strongholds you hold which are preventing your spiritual heart from being transformed?

Chapter 6 – Who We Were, Who We Are, and Who We Can Be

The phrase "spiritual heart" embraces the immaterial and material nature of humans. It is the repository of the *beliefs* and *values* which inform one's *expectations*, *emotions*, and observable *behaviors*. It represents the combined function of soul (eternal nature) and body (temporal nature).

In 2012, the Christian band *Big Daddy Weave* released a song entitled "Redeemed." The lyrics of the song include the phrase "I am not who I used to be."[15] When we accept the all-sufficient work of Jesus on our behalf, we are said to be a "new creation" (2 Cor 5:17 ESV). We are in fact no longer who we used to be—at least in our position in Christ from God's perspective. However, as we have seen in previous chapters, our daily experience does not immediately measure up to our position. We still possess a fallen nature until the day we die. There is a dichotomy. On the one hand, we have been redeemed. On the other hand, we are required to continually be transformed by the renewal of our minds (Rom 12:2)

---

[15] Big Daddy Weave. Lyrics to "Redeemed." ZionLyrics at https://zionlyrics.com/big-daddy-weave-redeemed-lyrics (accessed August 17, 2020).

and conformed to the image of Christ (Rom 8:29). Who we were, who we are, and who we can be is the dynamic through which we must navigate until the day we die.

The Dichotomy Within the Spiritual Heart

In addition to "strongholds," Paul uses another set of phrases to describe the condition of our spiritual hearts. Because of the fall in the Garden, a dichotomy exists in our spiritual hearts—a dichotomy between the spiritual heart consisting of distorted and largely anthropocentric *beliefs and behavior systems* versus the spiritual heart which consists of truth-based and Christo-centric *beliefs and behavior systems*. Paul contrasts the "old self" (Rom 6:6; Eph 4:22; Col 3:9) and "new self" (Eph 4:24; Col 3:10).

> We know that our **old self** was crucified with him in order that the body of sin might be brought to nothing, so that we would no longer be enslaved to sin. (Rom 6:6 ESV)
>
> To put off your **old self**, which belongs to your former manner of life and is corrupt through deceitful desires. (Eph 4:22 ESV)

> Do not lie to one another, seeing that you have put off the **old self** with its practices. (Col 3:9 ESV)
>
> And to put on the **new self**, created after the likeness of God in true righteousness and holiness. (Eph 4:24 ESV)
>
> And have put on the **new self**, which is being renewed in knowledge after the image of its creator. (Col 3:10 ESV)

The Problematic Dichotomy

The "old self" and "new self" phrases highlight the problematic dichotomy that is the basis of our spiritual struggle. As our *beliefs, values, expectations,* and *behaviors* are infused with internalized truth, the spiritual heart transforms with the renewal of the mind (Rom 12:2). There is conformity to the image of Jesus (Rom 8:29) as the "new self" emerges. When our *beliefs, values, expectations,* and *behaviors* have not been identified and acknowledged to be misaligned to truth and when there has been no repentance (change of mind/belief), the believer's immaterial, spiritual heart is described as the "old self".

The transformation and conformity of the spiritual heart from the "old self" to the "new self" is anything but instantaneous. The simplicity of that fact may cause us to overlook its profundity. While we are saints positionally in Christ when we place our trust in the all-sufficiency of His work, the grind of daily life often belies our saintly status. Why? It is simple. Our spiritual hearts desperately need transformation, renewal, and restoration. We live, maneuver, breathe, and operate in a spiritual war zone.

We do not exit the womb of spiritual rebirth immediately equipped to compete in this fallen world. Paul spoke to this reality when he exhorted his readers in Ephesus to "...*no longer walk as the Gentiles [unbelievers] do, in the futility of their minds*" (Eph 4:17 ESV). "Futility," the Greek word ματαιότης (*mataiotes*), pertains to "...being useless on the basis of being futile and lacking in content—'useless, futile, empty, futility.'"[16] It could thus be translated "emptiness"—a vacuum. Like a vacuum without a filter in a hazmat environment, our unprepared hearts become polluted with constant exposure to the marketplace of competing ideas and

---

[16] Johannes P. Louw and Eugene Albert Nida, *Greek-English Lexicon of the New Testament: Based on Semantic Domains* (New York: United Bible Societies, 1996), 624.

beliefs. If we remain spiritually passive or oblivious, the vacuum of our spiritual hearts fills with contaminated worldly ideologies and false *beliefs* which we accept to be true.

The dichotomy between our position in Christ on the one hand and the experiential outworking of our position on the other hand often confounds and bewilders us—as well as those who know and observe us. Christians amaze themselves and their observers with a dichotomy that is often labeled hypocrisy. The dichotomy between "new self" and "old self" in the *behavioral* manifestations of the spiritual heart is often a source of confusion to many. When we see only the "old self" on display through a person's behaviors, we may question whether they ever put their trust in Christ. Soteriological questions concerning the eternal security of the believer arise. Is Sam, who professes to be a believing Christian, evaluated in the public eye based upon his *behaviors* or based upon what and in Whom he has professed to *believe*? Maybe Sam has yet to fully "put off his old self." His *behaviors* do not align to the "new self" in Christ. Some judge Sam to be an unbeliever because of the dichotomy.

The pre-requisites for this transformation and conformation process include the *desire* to be all that God has called us to be in

Christ. In addition, objectivity, humility, and relevant truth are necessary. I've mentioned and described *desire* previously; however, objectivity, humility and relevant truth need some elaboration. It takes objectivity to be able to step outside of ourselves and consider how others and God evaluate our *behaviors*. It requires even greater objectivity for us to evaluate the *belief system complex* which underlies *behaviors*. A willingness to change, a repentant attitude, characterizes the humble person, the person who *desires* Christ to be glorified rather than self. Humility does not engage in *rationalization* and *justification behaviors* designed to preserve the status quo.

Finally, truth that is relevant to the *beliefs* associated with the specific *behaviors* is essential. For example, an understanding of the eschatological material in Revelation 20, while beneficial and relevant to one's understanding of the direction of God's redemptive program in human history, has little relevance to the biblical truths needed to deal with wounds to the spiritual heart inflicted by an abusive parent. In matters of spiritual heart restoration and renewal, critical distinctions exist between truths of a strategic nature that inform our philosophy of God's redemptive program in history and truths of a tactical nature which inform daily human relational matters. Both categories are of tremendous value and importance and do eventually intersect. Perhaps it has always been this way, but we are at a place in our culture today where the amount of instruction, counseling, and spiritual nurturing for wounded spiritual hearts suffering from various abuses, harmful influences, and addictions is so great that little time can be devoted to other categories of truth. It appears that as we move forward into the 21st Century, one of the biggest problems the church will face is mental and brain health. In many cases, this will be due to the increased prevalence of the very issues I've noted with the attendant impact or effect upon the spiritual heart.

Pain Accompanies Change

Conforming and transforming the spiritual heart from the "old self" to the "new self" does not occur without pain. Pain stimulates the desire to change. Pain accompanies change. There are two major categories of *motives* which underlie the development of the *beliefs* and *behaviors* we embrace:

† *Maximization of pleasure; avoidance of pain*—a natural, and to some extent, necessary motivation for physical

survival; however, when this is the primary motive for habituated *beliefs* and *behaviors*, the spiritual heart of the "old self" is anthropocentric.

† *Glorification of God* – a motive associated with *desires* to be transformed through the renewal of the mind and conformed to the image of Christ, thus necessary to the putting off of the "old self" and putting on the "new self". The spiritual heart of the "new self" in Christ is Christocentric.

Have you ever tried to change your routine so you could wake up an hour earlier to work out or have more quiet time with the Lord? Pain! Similarly, the "old self" will always pursue minimization of pain and maximization of perceived pleasure. These *beliefs* and *expectations* of the "old self" are not aligned to truth. The "old self" is our default mode—the path of least resistance. "Putting on the new self" is the path less taken, the road less traveled—the journey some of us never pursue or pursue only episodically. Paul refers to those of us in this category as "fleshly" or "natural" (1 Cor 2:14 to 3:3).

¹⁴ The **natural person** <u>does not accept</u> the things of the Spirit of God, for they are folly to him, and he is not able to understand them because they are spiritually discerned. ¹⁵ The **spiritual person** judges all things, but is himself to be judged by no one. ¹⁶ "For who has understood the mind of the Lord so as to instruct him?" But we have the mind of Christ.

3 But I, brothers, could not address you as **spiritual people**, but as **people of the flesh**, as infants in Christ. ² I fed you with milk, not solid food, for you were not ready for it. And even now you are not yet ready, ³ for you are still **of the flesh**. For while there is jealousy and strife among you, are you not **of the flesh** and behaving only in a human way? (1 Cor 2:14 to 3:3 ESV)

The anthropocentric *priorities and pursuits* of the "old self" are captured in synonyms such as "lovers of self", full of "selfish ambition", full of "self-indulgence" (2 Tim 3:2ff; Jas 3:14, 16; 5:5).

These synonyms reflect the dominant goals of minimization of pain and maximization of pleasure characteristic of the "old self."

For people will be **lovers of self**, lovers of money, proud, arrogant, abusive, disobedient to their parents, ungrateful, unholy, ³ heartless, unappeasable, slanderous, without self-control, brutal, not loving good, ⁴ treacherous, reckless, swollen with conceit, lovers of pleasure rather than lovers of God, ⁵ having the appearance of godliness, but denying its power. Avoid such people. (2 Tim 3:2–5 ESV)

But if you have bitter jealousy and selfish ambition in your hearts, do not boast and be false to the truth. (Jas 3:14 ESV)

For where jealousy and **selfish ambition** exist, there will be disorder and every vile practice. (Jas 3:16 ESV)

You have lived on the earth in luxury and in **self-indulgence**. You have fattened your hearts in a day of slaughter. (Jas 5:5 ESV)

At some point, and perhaps even now, we've all been there. But, we have hope. We can rise above the spiritual abnormality of our fallen state. It is not normal. We can aspire to a live consistently in the "new self." God gives us time. He knows time is needed to learn relevant biblical truths necessary for transformation (Rom 12:2) and spiritual conformity to the image of Jesus (Rom 8:29), the aspirational objectives of the believer. The following list contains some questions which I have found helpful in discerning and distinguishing "old self" and "new self".

† Do I rationalize and justify my *behaviors* to myself? To others?

† Do I look for opportunities to extend mercy, grace and love to others *motivated* by what God has done for me?

† How thankful on a daily basis am I for God's patience and longsuffering?

† Are there any people who enable me in any addictions or other habituated *behaviors* not aligned with truth?

† How do my verbal interactions with others align to Colossians 4:6?

> Let your speech always be gracious, seasoned with salt, so that you may know how you ought to answer each person. (Col 4:6 ESV)

† Do I have *beliefs* about my identity which are shaped more by harmful experiences (e.g. what others have said or done to me) instead of the way God sees me? If so, how are those *beliefs* affecting my *values, expectations,* and my *behaviors*—my *relational strategies*, my *rationales and justifications*, my *self-talk*, my *verbal engagement with others*, my *pursuits and priorities?*

† How do I spend my time and money? These are two indicators of *pursuits and priorities.*

To summarize, the phrase "old self" encapsulates the anthropocentric orientation of the spiritual heart's *beliefs, expectations,* and *behavior* complex. The phrase "new self" encapsulates a Christocentric orientation of the spiritual heart. If we grasp the significance of the meaning of these phrases, we grasp what will be vital to understanding the spiritual heart condition and solution process.

Once we understand the importance of these concepts, we read a passage like Ephesians 3:14–19 through a different lens.

> [14] For this reason I bow my knees before the Father, [15] from whom every family in heaven and on earth is named, [16] that according to the riches of his glory he may grant you to be strengthened with power through his Spirit in your **inner being**, [17] so that **Christ may dwell in your hearts** through **faith**—that you, being rooted and grounded in love, [18] may have strength to comprehend with all the saints what is the breadth and length and height and depth, [19] and **to know the love of Christ** that surpasses knowledge, that you may be **filled with all the fullness of God.** (Eph 3:14–19 ESV)

We will address the Holy Spirit in the next chapter; however, did you read this passage and grasp the significance of Paul's statements in a new way? Note the phrases and terms "*inner being*", "*Christ may dwell in your hearts*", and "*through faith.*" We exercise faith in what we *believe*. Christ only dwells in the spiritual heart which is infused with the truth. There is no lie in truth and there is no lie where Christ abides and dwells. The love of Christ in our spiritual heart is beyond mere knowledge. The spiritual heart undergoing transformation, renewal, and restoration is where Christ can dwell and surpass mere knowledge or intellectual assent. As this transformational process progresses, our spiritual hearts fill with the fullness of God.

Speaking of the "fullness of God," what about being filled with the Holy Spirit? How do the "fullness of God," being "filled with the Holy Spirit," the "new self," and the spiritually healthy, spiritual heart relate to each other? I devote the next two chapters to an attempt to address these questions. First, we need to get some biblical clarity regarding the phrase "filled with the Holy Spirit."

Questions for Consideration:
- † How would you define the relationship between the spiritual heart and the "old self" and "new self" mentioned by Paul?
- † There were two categories of motive mentioned – maximization of pleasure/avoidance of pain and the

glorification of God. Which motive dominates the majority of people's lives?

Chapter 7 – The Best Helper

The phrase "spiritual heart" embraces the immaterial and material nature of humans. It is the repository of the *beliefs* and *values* which inform one's *expectations, emotions*, and observable *behaviors*. It represents the combined function of soul (eternal nature) and body (temporal nature).

The sea of notions teems with proposed meanings of what being "filled with the Holy Spirit" means. Flotation devices are definitely needed. Many ships have wrecked in these waters. Have you ever asked five or ten people to define the "filling with the Holy Spirit?" Just as an experiment, try it sometime. Then, also ask them if they would mind giving two or three ways we know when we are "filled with the Holy Spirit." Keep a mental or perhaps physical log of the definitions and descriptions you hear. The purpose of this exercise is not to embarrass or make light of anyone. It is certainly not for the purpose of displaying some arrogant superior knowledge (1 Cor 8:1). The exercise is enlightening regarding the various views, perspectives and understandings that exist in the Christian marketplace of ideas. Because of the ambiguity, do we just dismiss this important phrase and concept as another topic which we should avoid? After all, there seem to be different views and little understanding of the difference it makes anyway. Personally, if there is an explanation that makes sense, we want to know about it. If you are like me, I'd rather swim through the sea of notions than remain adrift on it. I think we can reach some clarity.

The Divine Helper

God provides divine power in our spiritual journey of heart transformation, renewal, and restoration. As we've noted so often, we are charged with a goal of transformation through the renewal of our minds (Rom 12:2) and conformity to the image of Christ (Rom 8:29). The *belief/behavior system complex* which is central to the spiritual heart is the locus of this activity.

The Holy Spirit indwells the believer (e.g. Rom 8:9, 11; 1 Cor 3:16; 2 Tm 1:14), but there is a "filling" with the Holy Spirit (e.g. Acts 2:4; 9:17; 13:9; Eph 5:18) and there is also a ministerial function of the Holy Spirit to the believer (Rom 8:16). These are three separate, but related Holy Spirit phenomenon. While this is not a book on pneumatology, I need to briefly address these distinctions as we introduce the role of the Holy Spirit in our spiritual heart transformation, renewal, and restoration process. Believers of the present age and the future kingdom age (millennium) are (and will be) permanently indwelt by the Holy Spirit. We enjoy this privilege in distinction from believers of prior ages.

The Divine Helper in Prior Ages

In prior ages, God gave the Holy Spirit to select individuals for a God-sanctioned purpose. Once the purpose was accomplished, He withdrew the Holy Spirit. The duration of this enduement or "filling" of the Holy Spirit varied. We find the following examples in Scripture:

- † The artisans were filled with the Spirit of God to enable them to design and make all of the artistry and accouterments of the Tabernacle (Ex 31:3; 35:31)
- † Balaam's oracle of blessing intended for cursing was given to him when the Spirit of God came upon him (Nm 24:2–3)
- † The Judges of Israel were empowered by the Spirit for ruling and conducting military engagements (Jgs 3:9–10; 11:29; 13:25; 14:6, 19; 15:14)

- † The Spirit of God enabled Saul to prophesy when Samuel anointed him (1 Sm 10:10)
- † The Spirit of God empowered Saul to defeat the Ammonites (1 Sm 11:6)
- † The Spirit of the Lord departed from Saul when God rejected him as king and appointed David (1 Sm 16:13–14)
- † The messengers whom Saul sent to take David end up prophesying when the Spirit of God comes upon them (1 Sm 19:20, 23)
- † David acknowledges that "the Spirit of the Lord speaks" by him (2 Sm 23:2)
- † David prays that God not take the Holy Spirit from him (Ps 51:11)

During the later portion of this prior age, the portion of the age of Israel in which Jesus' incarnation and public ministry occurred, a "filling with" or "by the Holy Spirit" akin to the enduement or filling also occurred.

- † The angel of the Lord appears to Zechariah and tells him that his and Elizabeth's son, John, will be "...*filled with the Holy Spirit, even from his mother's womb*" (Lk 1:15)

- Elizabeth is *"filled with the Holy Spirit"* as she prophesies and blesses Mary (Lk 1:41)
- Zechariah is *"filled with the Holy Spirit"* as he prophesies at the birth of John (Lk 1:67)
- Jesus is said to be *"full of the Holy Spirit"* when He was led into the wilderness for forty days of temptation by Satan (Lk 4:1–2)

So, throughout the historical age of Israel, the enduement or "filling" of the Holy Spirit was a phenomenon experienced by select believers for specific, God-sanctioned purposes and activities. This filling was temporary in contrast to the "indwelling" previously noted.

The Divine Helper During the Transition Period of the First Century A.D.

During the transition period addressed in the book of Acts and, in particular during the period from Pentecost through the midst of Paul's first missionary journey, select groups of believers experienced a *"filling"* of the Holy Spirit which was related to some activity, service or spiritual production. These "filling" occurrences ranged from the speaking in other, known languages at Pentecost (Acts 2:4) to the disciples being *"filled with joy and with the Holy Spirit"* in the midst of persecution (Acts 13:50–52). Other examples include Acts 4:8, 31; 6:3, 5; 7:55; 9:17; 11:24; 13:9, 52. The last recorded instance of a believer being *"filled"* with the Holy Spirit during this period is recorded in Acts 13:52. So, the biblical account of the Holy Spirit's engagement in the lives of humans up to approximately A.D. 49 when Paul concluded his first missionary journey is one in which the Holy Spirit endues or fills select individuals or groups of people for specific purposes.

The Divine Helper Permanently Indwells and Ministers – Content of "Filling" Changes

As we previously noted, Paul will indicate that the Holy Spirit indwells believers in a permanent sense (Rom 8:9, 11; 1 Cor 3:16; 2 Tm 1:14). He also indicates that the Holy Spirit "sealed" believers which is a synonym for indwelling (2 Cor 1:22; Eph 1:13; 4:30). This indwelling of the Holy Spirit will also be a spiritual asset and privilege of the future kingdom age. It is promised to the believer of the kingdom age when the ultimate descendant of David,

Jesus, reigns as a part of the fulfillment of God's covenant with Abraham (Gn 12:1–3 cf. Jl 2:28–32; Is 32:15–18; 44:3; Ez 36:26–27; cf. Jn 7:37–39; 14:15–18; 15:13, 26; 16:5–15).

One more passage in the New Testament references a *"filling"* with the Spirit. In Ephesians 5:18, Paul writes "Do not get drunk with wine, for that is debauchery, but be filled with the Spirit." Paul does not refer to some past event nor some future period here. Rather, he commands it. He exhorts believers to be filled. But, wait! What Paul commands in this passage is different.

Previously, God selected which individuals experienced a filling with the Holy Spirit. Here, believers have control over the filling—a matter of the volition. Paul wrote Ephesians in the early A.D. 60's. This contrasts sharply with the last recorded incident of filling in Acts 13:52 around A.D. 49—a difference of thirteen to fifteen years.

There is more involved here that is beyond the scope and focus of this book, but for our purposes, Paul exhorts believers in regard to what should be the norm in the Christian experience from that time forward. This *"filling"* differs drastically. Paul commands the believer to be filled with content different from the Holy Spirit even though the Holy Spirit will have a role to play in the process.

The "*filling*" Paul commands in Ephesians 5:18 should not be conflated with the "*filling*" observed in the Old Testament nor the Gospel of Luke and the Acts narrative. Paul exhorts his readers in Ephesians 5:18 to be "filled" with the content of the character of God or Christ.

The Importance and Relevance of the Holy Spirit and the Spiritual Heart

Why again is this topic important and why am I addressing it? The Holy Spirit is vital to the renewal, restoration and transformation process of the spiritual heart. In order for us to reach the shore of clarity, we must navigate our way through the sea of notions. If our notions (*beliefs*) include the Holy Spirit doing something for us based upon how He interacted in the past or future with people under a different administrative phase of God's redemptive program, we possess unrealistic *expectations*. These unrealistic *expectations* rest upon a foundation of incorrect *beliefs*.

Clarifying the Understanding of the Helper for Us Today

How then should we understand Paul's exhortation or command in Ephesians 5:18? In his *Greek Grammar: Beyond the Basics*, Dr. Daniel Wallace provides helpful insight into the Greek text which underlies our English translations. The English translations easily enable shallow observation which often leads to a conflation of Ephesians 5:18 with other passages that mention a "*filling*" of the Holy Spirit.

In all of the instances in Luke's Gospel and in the Acts account where we find a "*filling*" with or a "*full of*" the Holy Spirit (Lk 1:15, 41, 67; 4:1; Acts 2:4; 4:8, 31; 6:3, 5; 7:55; 9:17; 11:24; 13:9, 52), the Greek phrase uses a genitive case—a noun case that indicates content. The content is the Holy Spirit, poured, as it were, into these people and the Holy Spirit produces an outcome—a service or activity—in their lives . When we transport these passages out of their historical context and conflate the meaning and the experience of the people in these passages to us, we remain adrift on the sea of notions.

The *belief that* being "filled" with the Holy Spirit in the same sense as those who are the subject of these passages produces an *expectation* of a supernatural empowering phenomenon upon which we need to wait. This expectation makes sense when we observe the "filling" with the content of the Holy Spirit mentioned in the Luke, Acts and Old Testament passages. Note the characteristics of this "filling" which is last noted to have occurred in Acts 13:52.

† The subjects in these passages did not ask for this type of filling nor is it commanded of them

† It was a complete filling; not partial

† It was instantaneous, not progressive or the result of ongoing experiential sanctification in a person's life

† They did not pray to receive it

† It is not associated with discerning the will of God for their lives.

† In fact, the Scriptural evidence indicates that only select individuals and groups experienced this type of filling.

Commenting on Acts 2:4, Wallace's observations and insights prove helpful and instructive.

> It is to be noted that neither the verb nor the case following the verb are the same as in Eph 5:18…The command there to be filled by the Spirit

has nothing to do with tongues-speaking. The Spirit-filling (with πίμπλημι) in Acts is <u>never commanded, nor is it related particularly to sanctification</u>. Rather, <u>it is a special imbueing of the Spirit for a particular task</u> (similar to the Spirit's ministry in the OT). Furthermore, every time the case is used to indicate the content of filling is the gen., never the dat. Cf. Acts 4:8, 31; 9:17; 13:9 (cf. also Luke 1:15, 41).[17]

The contrast between the Luke, Acts, and Old Testament passages with the special "filling" of the Holy Spirit could not present a more stark contrast with what Paul commands in Ephesians 5:18. Again, note the observations and insights provided by Wallace.

> <u>One of the most misunderstood passages</u> in the NT is Eph 5:18, where πληρόω is followed by (ἐν) πνεύματι. A <u>typical translation</u> is "be filled with the Spirit" which <u>implies that the Spirit is the content</u>

---

[17] Daniel B. Wallace, *Greek Grammar Beyond the Basics* (Grand Rapids, Michigan: Zondervan Publishing, 1996), 94. (Underlining is mine for emphasis).

of the filling. But this is highly suspect from the Greek point of view.[18]

To see ἐν πνεύματι here as indicating content is grammatically suspect (even though it is, in many circles, the predominant view). Only if the flow of argument and/or the lack of other good possibilities strongly point in the direction of content would we be compelled to take it as such. There are no other examples in biblical Greek in which ἐν + the dative after πληρόω indicates content. Further, the parallel with οἴνῳ as well as the common grammatical category of *means* suggest that the idea intended is that believers are to be filled *by means of* the [Holy] Spirit. It so, there seems to be an unnamed agent.

The meaning of this text can only be appreciated in light of the πληρόω language in Ephesians. Always the term is used in connection with a member of the

---

[18] Ibid., 93. (Underlining is mine for emphasis).

Trinity. Three considerations seem to be key: (1) In Eph 3:19 the "hinge" prayer introducing the last half of the letter makes a request that the believers "be filled with all the fullness of God" (πληρωθῆτε εἰς πᾶν τὸ πλήρωμα τοῦ θεοῦ). The explicit *content* of πληρόω is thus God's fullness (probably a reference to his moral attributes). (2) In 4:10 Christ is said to be the agent of filling (with v 11 adding the specifics of his giving spiritual gifts). (3) The author then brings his argument to a crescendo in 5:18: Believers are to be filled by Christ by means of the Spirit with the content of the fullness of God.[19]

This "filling" with the content of the fullness of God has everything to do with spiritual heart renewal, restoration, and transformation. The fact that Paul is exhorting believers to be so filled indicates that it is a product of our volitional choice. A summary of observations aided by Dr. Wallace's analysis about the "filling" of Ephesians 5:18 provides a stark contrast to the "filling"

---

[19] Ibid., 375.

of the Holy Spirit we have seen in the Luke and Acts passages. Briefly, we observe the following.

- † The "filling" of Ephesians 5:18 is not instantaneous
- † It is associated with experiential sanctification, thus it is progressive in nature and attained partially or incrementally over time
- † The character of God is the content of this filling—not the Holy Spirit.

We shall examine what having the character of God in our spiritual hearts looks like in the next chapter, but suffice it to say for now that even though the Holy Spirit has a role to play in this process, the "*filling of the Holy Spirit*" for us today looks nothing like the experience of the "*fillings with the Holy Spirit*" of Luke, Acts, and the Old Testament. Our spiritual hearts are actively engaged in the Ephesians 5:18 process as our *belief/behavior complex* is adjusted to the character of God incrementally and progressively if we pursue Paul's exhortation. We should not be waiting for some outpouring experience of the Holy Spirit to propel us forward. The following visual attempts to represent the difference highlighted here.

Filling with the Holy Spirit as the Content
(OT, Luke, and Acts)

Filling with the Character of Christ
(Ephesians 5:18)

So Today, What Does the Helper Holy Spirit Do?

What then is the role of the Holy Spirit in this "filling" with the content of the character of God? Obviously, our volitional choices play a critical role in this process, but how is the Holy Spirit engaged? He teaches us (1 Cor 2:12 cf. 1 Jn 2:27); leads us (Rom 8:14); witnesses with our spirits (Rom 8:16); and makes intercession for us (Rom 8:26–27). These are subjective activities by the Holy Spirit. They are specific to each believer. We can hinder these activities of the Holy Spirit.

> Christian character is a divine product which is not to be realized but partially and that at the end of a painful self-effort, as is the case with the world in using its method, but is a product which becomes wholly and instantly available when right relation to the Holy Spirit <u>is unhindered</u>.[20]

The transformation of our spiritual hearts infuses the character of God made manifest in observable ways known as the

---

[20] Lewis S. Chafer, *Chafer Systematic Theology,* vol. 6, *Pneumatology* (Dallas, Texas: Dallas Seminary Press, 1948, renewed 1975), 201. (Underlining is mine for emphasis).

fruit of the Spirit (Gal 5:22–24). The Holy Spirit ministers to us, but spiritual heart transformation leads to filling with the character of God. Unrealistic *expectations* regarding the *"filling with the Holy Spirit"* leave us adrift on the sea of notions without a rudder and without direction. The notion (*belief*) that a supernatural, Holy Spirit experience awaits somewhere just over the horizon which will guide us safely to the shore of clarity fogs the truth and leaves us adrift on the sea of notions. Paul's prayer for the believers in Ephesus perfectly incorporates these concepts I have been addressing related to the spiritual heart transformation, empowerment of the Holy Spirit, character of God, and conformity to the image of Christ.

> [14] For this reason I bow my knees before the Father, [15] from whom every family in heaven and on earth is named, [16] that according to the riches of his glory he may grant you to be <u>strengthened with power through his Spirit in your inner being</u>, [17] so that <u>Christ may dwell in your hearts</u> through faith—that you, being rooted and grounded in love, [18] <u>may have strength</u> to comprehend with all the saints

what is the breadth and length and height and depth, [19] and <u>to know the love of Christ</u> that surpasses knowledge, that you may be <u>filled with all the fullness of God</u>. [20] Now to him who is able to do far more abundantly than all that we ask or think, according to the power at work within us, [21] to him be glory in the church and in Christ Jesus throughout all generations, forever and ever. Amen. (Eph 3:14–21 ESV)

Wow! I hope we see this passage differently now. If so, we may be closer to grasping all that is contained in those few verses. In fact, the Bible is packed with insight regarding the spiritual heart of the believer and the process of restoration, renewal and transformation. How is this transformation accomplished? How is the spiritual heart persona of the "old self" transformed so that we "put on the new self" which reflects the character of God/Christ through the fruit of the Spirit? What does such a spiritual heart look like? Let's take a look.

Questions for Consideration:

- † What are some common notions about the "filling of the Holy Spirit?"
- † How would you define the "filling with the Holy Spirit" after reading this chapter?
- † With what are we to be filled according to Ephesians 5:18? What role does the spiritual heart play in this?

Chapter 8 – When Hearts Align

The phrase "spiritual heart" embraces the immaterial and material nature of humans. It is the repository of the *beliefs* and *values* which inform one's *expectations*, *emotions*, and observable *behaviors*. It represents the combined function of soul (eternal nature) and body (temporal nature).

In 1975, Jefferson Starship released an album entitled *Red Octopus*. One of the hit songs on the album was "Miracles." It is now a classic and conjures nostalgic memories and feelings in the romantic hearts of any who were at the prime of their teens and twenties during the '70's. I graduated from High School in 1975 and remember listening to this song on the AM radio in my 1963 Chevy Nova SS with bucket seats as I entered college that Fall. It is a good thing that my AM radio did not provide the clarity of modern-day earbuds and podcast players. Some of the lyrics of the long version are sensuous even by today's standards. The lyrics I do recall included phrases like "if only you believe like I believe, baby we'd get by" and "but from that first look in your eyes I knew you and I had but one heart."[21] Two people, one heart, shared beliefs. Wow! We dream of having that type of relationship with a spouse. That *desire* on the human level driven by God-given *needs* is only exceeded by what God desires with us. God desires our heart to be aligned with His heart. If only we *believed* like He wants us to *believe*, we'd more than get by. Our spiritual hearts would be transformed and our relationship with Him would thrive and flourish.

What God Wants Us to Believe for Our Hearts to Align to His Heart

God desires that our hearts align to His heart. He wants us to see ourselves through His eyes of truth, not the lies about ourselves, God, our relationships, and wrong viewpoints that we have believed. The "old self" (Rom 6:6; Eph 4:22; Col 3:9) versus "new self" (Eph 4:24; Col 3:10) dichotomy contrasts two conflicting versions of the spiritual heart. God views the "old self" to have been crucified with Christ (Rom 6:6 cf. Col 3:9). Obviously, we were not there with Jesus on the Cross in an experiential sense.

---

[21] Jefferson Starship. 1975. *Red Octopus*, "Miracles." LyricsFreak https://www.lyricsfreak.com/j/jefferson+starship/miracles_20070383.html accessed August 18, 2020.

Our "old-self" was placed on the Cross with Christ in position. Similarly, in position, we have a "new self" that was resurrected with Christ (Col 3:1). These positional and spiritual realities are the basis for our experiential aspirations in time even while we still possess a fallen nature.

Aligning Our Heart to God's Heart: Making Positional Truth an Experiential Reality

The reality of our fallen nature imprints itself upon our spiritual hearts in ways that take a lifetime to unpack. If we are to strive toward the aspirational objectives of spiritual heart transformation and restoration, we need to understand how to make that which is true of us in position to be an experiential reality. How do we become "filled with all the fullness of God" (Eph 3:19)? How do our spiritual hearts become infused with the character of God and Christ?

The "old self" is a persona or a personification of our spiritual heart built around a core of an anthropocentric *belief/behavior system.* The primary dual goals of pain avoidance and pleasure maximization dominate the *motivations* of the "old self."

Don't beat yourself up for having an old self. That would be like beating the tiger because he has stripes or getting angry at the fish because it prefers water. God knows our predicament as fallen humans. We are also surrounded by and come into contact daily with others who have an "old self." Their verbal and other behaviors reflect it too—as do ours to the extent we have not "put off" the old self.

We Construct the "Old Self" Over Time – Consciously and Unconsciously

We construct the "old self" in our spiritual hearts over time with a conscious layer and an unconscious layer. *Beliefs, values, expectations,* and *behavior systems* are inherent to the "old self." Sometimes, we absorb them unconsciously, such as through exposure in early childhood to what parents say and what we observe around us. Oblivious to what is happening in our spiritual hearts, a child absorbs what a parent says about other people—what they say about those in authority, those under their authority, friends, money, their status relative to others, their opinion about different occupations, politics, etc. Even as adults, we unconsciously absorb *beliefs*, *values*, *expectations*, and *behavior systems* through our culture, media, academia, and society at large. For instance, consider how much social media influences and is shaping us individually and socially in each of these components of our spiritual hearts. Once we see a view or *belief* promoted or posted incessantly on social media platforms, we begin to accept it as fact or as truth. Even if two days later, it is proven to not be true, it is too late. In the early 21st Century, perception is reality—not just as a saying, it really is "truth." Once accepted, a retraction or correction goes virtually unnoticed. It is buried by the subsequent deluge of information that crowds out any application of critical thinking and objective analysis. We really do live in a "post-truth" world where "truth" is something external that we need to appropriate. We are the final arbiters of "truth" and you have yours and I have mine. We have become our own gods.

    The "old self" gets constructed in quasi-unconscious ways as well. For instance, you and I probably know (or have experienced ourselves) the direct assault upon our spiritual hearts, our *beliefs* about our identity, who we are and of what value we are, resulting from a parent saying something like "you are stupid" or "you will never be worth anything" or some harmful comment about physical appearance. Those are wounds to the spiritual heart which go deep—even into the sub-consciousness where they may be repressed. Perhaps worse even still are the wounds to the spiritual heart resulting from physical or sexual abuse.

We also construct some "old self" *belief/behavior systems* of the spiritual heart in a more conscious manner, i.e. philosophies or ideologies we embrace to be truth which may or may not be aligned with the final arbiter of all truth, the Bible. The *belief/behavior systems* of the spiritual heart impacted by any of these examples at the conscious and unconscious layers are not just common, they are prolific. They are the "old self" and an unavoidable reality of human existence in this fallen world.

The Trial and Error Process of "Old Self" Development and Refinement

As we move forward from childhood to adolescence to adults, we develop *belief/behavior systems* through a process of trial and error. Some of the individual *beliefs* may align to values and principles that are truth-based. For instance, many people embrace *beliefs* and *values* consistent with some degree of truth regarding the importance of the family, principles of leadership, God, work, treating others fairly, etc. while at the same time they embrace *beliefs*, *values*, *expectations*, and *relational strategies* at odds with the truth of Scripture. Have you ever known a church-going and loving husband and father who was a politico in the corporate realm? The distinguishing element between the "old self" and "new self" when truth-based *values* and principles are present in the *beliefs* of the spiritual heart is this. Are your primary *motivations* or goals anthropocentric or Christocentric? Are we seeking self-glorification and notoriety or are we seeking Christ exaltation? The "old self" has its origins in the fall in the Garden—"for God knows that when you eat of it your eyes will be opened, and you will be like God..." (Gn 3:5 ESV).

At the most basic level, during the trial and error process, we reject or refine our *belief/behavior system* as needed in order to achieve our definition of success. To the extent that our *beliefs* about our identity relates to abuse or the negative lens formed by the harmful statements of others, we are more likely to have guilt, shame, or a *desire* to hide our past from others. We *expect* that others will view us the same way.

The person who has suffered some type of abuse and has a poor self-identity may hide behind any number of *behavior* patterns as a part of their "old self" coping *relational strategies*. (See chapter 4). For the rest of us who do not have that type of trauma as a part of our past, we still follow the same script as we embrace *belief/behavior systems*, try them, adjust them, refine them, or reject and replace them. But, in the end, all we are doing is building an "old self" persona that is not *"filled with the fullness of God"* or *"conformed to the image of Christ."* Whatever temporal happiness we may attain as a result of our "success," we find ourselves lacking permanent contentment and joy. We encase our spiritual hears in strongholds (chapter 5) and a hardened heart of our own variety.

The Good News – Restoration and Renewal of the "New Self"

Good news! God uses our failure and our lack of contentment to get our attention and recognize that we are hopeless, helpless, and completely dependent upon Him. Our independent "old self" begins to crumble under the pressure of suffering and joyless existence—if not under even greater pressures.

In order to *"put on the new self"* experientially in our lives, we must know the identity of the One into whose image we are to be conformed. When I was a child and adolescent, I absorbed a *belief system* related to my identity which, like a lot of people, reflected a lower value of myself than others. It was not based upon any particular abuse. My "old self" identity formed based upon the dynamics of my childhood environment, influences such as my parent's perspectives of their status , accomplishments relative to others, and a number of other factors. As a coping and compensating mechanism, I became a driven student and a perfectionist to a flaw. I pursued Judo outside of my school system even though I could have probably been a decent basketball player as I had a really good jump shot—but not the best. It wasn't perfect. I did not fully realize why I viewed my identity the way I did until many years later.

Unknowingly, I was primarily anthropocentric in my identity search. I was looking for a human role model of success I could emulate. Why? A young person looks for a successful role model to emulate at least in part because he or she is searching for an acceptable identity. I wish a Christian mentor could have pulled me aside and encouraged me to not look for any human to emulate but showed me examples of what emulating Jesus in my relationships with others really looked like. I mean—not just doing good deeds, but being the example myself whom others could emulate. What does the character of God look like in a genuine, authentic way in a young adult in their teens and twenties? If that person, that mentor, had told me that by looking for another fallen human to emulate, I was de-valuing myself, what a vision that would have provided me. I was getting academic information in school and church and I attempted to master the knowledge to a tee. What I needed was instruction in what all of that knowledge looked like in practice. How does a Christocentric leader motivate, influence, and set the example in personal relationships, in social settings, in competitive environments, in corporations and the workplace, and in the church? It has taken me years to learn (and I am still learning) how to identify the "old self" *motivations* that are anthropocentric and seeking some degree of self-exaltation. It has taken me just as long to learn how to replace those "old self" *beliefs, values, motivations,* and *behaviors* with the "new self" that resembles something more akin to Christ. I still have a long way to go and the process will continue until the day I die.

God does not desire you or me to be anyone but you or me. He values each of us for who we are and desires us to become our full potential—a potential only realized in Him, in becoming full of Him, His character. That is transformative stuff. The realization that we could actually be a channel through which He might bless others provides our lives immense value, purpose, definition, and a framework. You and I can actually say things that might impact others in a positive way—for time and eternity. I could actually do things which might change another person's life trajectory. I could be the one who actually lifts someone up instead of looking to a role model to lift me up. Our identity, how we define ourselves as Christians, is crucial. Our definition of our identity reflects our *beliefs* about who and what we are and our understanding of God. Until we "put on the new self," the identity of the "old self" will be woven into the fabric of our spiritual hearts.

The "new self" personifies a *belief/behavior system* that has as its central defining purpose the glorification of Christ in and through our life. It is Christocentric. Our *desires, motivations, mental behaviors, verbal behaviors, relational patterns and strategies,* and *priorities and pursuits* require alignment to truth-based *beliefs* and *values.* "Old self" beliefs underlie our anthropocentric identities. Christocentric realities underpin our "new self" identity.

The Process – Putting Off the "Old Self" and Putting On the "New Self"

What does the process of putting off the "old self" and putting on the "new self" look like? Paul provides insightful guidance in Romans 6. This chapter encapsulates a theme which threads its way through all of Paul's letters and epistles—know that which is true of you positionally in Christ and make it experiential in your life.

In Romans 6:1–4, Paul asks his readers several questions which should remind them of the realities of their spiritual position in Christ.

> What shall we say then? Are we to continue in sin that grace may abound? [2] By no means! How can we who died to sin still live in it? [3] Do you not know that all of us who have been baptized into

Christ Jesus were baptized into his death? ⁴ We were buried therefore with him by baptism into death, in order that, just as Christ was raised from the dead by the glory of the Father, we too might walk in newness of life. (Rom 6:1–4 ESV)

In verse 1, Paul poses a question about our <u>experience</u> – "*Are we to continue in sin that grace may abound?*" In verses 2–4a, Paul poses questions designed to remind his readers of spiritual realities due to their <u>position</u> in Christ. We have not experienced any of the things Paul mentions in our physical bodies. We have not <u>experienced</u> a physical baptism into Jesus' death, nor a physical resurrection. Yet, Paul writes to his audience as if they should know these things to be true of them—in position, not in actual, physical experience.

At the end of verse 4, Paul provides the reason—so that "*...we too might walk in newness of life.*" This is a reference to the "new self." In verse 5, he reminds his readers of their ultimate destiny which is to be resurrected like Him—"*...we shall certainly be united with him in a resurrection like his.*" Then, in verse 6, Paul builds upon these truths and describes a process that continues until verse 13.

† First, the process is built upon the foundation of *beliefs*—**knowing** that our "old self" was put to death with Christ for a purpose—that we would no longer be slaves to sin (v. 6). This knowledge includes the fact that we will live with Him in resurrected bodies (vv. 7–10 cf. Col 3:1–4).

† Second, we **consider** ourselves dead to sin, particularly the "old self," and alive to God in Christ, the "new self" (v. 11). This *"considering"* refers to the internalization of truth whereby we make truth our own. Internalized truth infuses our spiritual hearts rather than remaining a body of academic information to be adored panoramically like a beautiful library. We own it. It is our *beliefs*, our *values*. Internalized truth is foundational to replacing the product of sin, the "old self" (v. 12).

† Third, we **present** our members to God "…as instruments of righteousness" (v. 13). Our members are our spiritual hearts and bodies, including our brain with all of its neural pathways where habituated patterns have been constructed as the "old self."

So, in summary, this process consists of **knowing** truth, **internalizing** truth, and **presenting** our members to God Who is truth. As we habituate this pattern, our brains have neuroplasticity and new pathways will form in place of the old. Neuroplasticity highlights the incredibly interwoven and interconnected nature of our spiritual hearts and body. Even the addiction-laden "old self" can be transformed beginning with the renewal of the mind through the internalization of truth. Paul, under the inspiration of the Holy Spirit, knew what he was talking about when he wrote Romans 12:2. Science has only added validation of the truth of Scripture.

What is Spiritual Maturity Then?

What is spiritual maturity and how does that concept relate to the transformation journey of the spiritual heart? Spiritual maturity is tantamount to the biblical concept of "perfection" (Rom 12:2 cf. Mt 5:48) whereby the believer is "yielding to" or "presenting" his/her members (mind, body, soul, spiritual heart) to internalized truth consistently. We never reach a perfected state in this life in which further transformation is not possible. Jesus never had an "old self" since He never possessed a fallen nature and never sinned. But if anyone had ever reached the ultimate status of spiritual "arrival," it would have been the apostle Paul.

Paul provides us with critical insight into what spiritual maturity means in view of the fact that spiritual heart transformation is a continual process in this life. Note that Paul was **still pursuing** the **aspirational goal** of transformation of the mind (Rom 12:2) and conformity to the image of Jesus (Rom 8:29) through the **process** he embedded in Romans 6 and had still yet to "attain" full conformity or "perfection" just a few short years prior to his death.

> [12] <u>Not that I have already obtained this or am already perfect</u>, but <u>I press on to make it my own</u>, because Christ Jesus has made me his own. [13] Brothers, <u>I do not consider that I have made it my own</u>. But one thing I do: forgetting what lies behind and straining forward to what lies ahead, [14] I press on toward the goal for the prize of the upward call of God in Christ Jesus. [15] <u>Let those of us who are mature think this way</u>, and if in anything you think otherwise, God will reveal that also to you. [16] Only let us hold true to what we have attained. (Phil 3:12–16 ESV)

This is so encouraging. Paul, like Jesus, a man around whose ministry human history pivots, acknowledges his continued pressing on toward the objective, the "*…upward call of God in Christ Jesus.*" This is just another way of saying "*conformity to the image of Christ*" or becoming the "*fullness of Christ.*" When in verse 12, Paul indicates that he has not "*already obtained this*" and that he was pressing on to make "*it*" his own, Paul is referencing the experiential realization in his life of a positional reality. Paul had yet to fully incorporate the positional realities of co-crucifixion and co-resurrection with Christ into his experience in this life. Paul's prevalent theme emerges yet again.

What is it like to internalize God's view of our "old self" as crucified with Christ? As we subject our "old self" to crucifixion, our "new self" is progressively being resurrected. Resurrection of the "new self" springs forth from crucifixion of the "old self." That is Paul's reference point (cf. v. 11). Amazing isn't it? Yet, even Paul acknowledges that the fullest attainment of transformation and conformity to Christ's image occurs only when we pass into His presence and experience the resurrection as He did for all eternity.

What Our Hearts Look Like When Aligned to God's Heart

So, are there some characteristics of the spiritual heart aligned to God's heart that we can summarize? I have found the following to be helpful.

- † When our spiritual hearts align to God's heart, momentum is <u>continued</u> and <u>consistent</u> in the putting off of the "old self" and putting on of the "new self"—not episodic and sporadic. Just a note of encouragement—as we begin this journey, the process and steps discussed in this book will likely be episodic and sporadic—perhaps for years or longer. Relax. It happens to everyone who strives for continuity and consistency in the journey—probably more than once. However, never settle for episodic and sporadic.
- † The alignment of our spiritual hearts to Jesus and truth is an ongoing process until we enter eternity. I believe we will even continue to grow in eternity. After all, God is infinite and we are not. But that is not our focus now.
- † There is no magical or instantaneous path.
- † No supernatural "filling with the Holy Spirit" looms over the horizon to magically transform us.

- † The path becomes increasingly less trodden and perhaps even lonely the further along it we journey. Consider Paul's final year of life in prison.
- † The joy and contentment we experience along this path provides peace and assurance within a spiritual heart that is trusting in Him and adjusted to truth.
- † We experience wholeness or integrity in the spiritual heart—an alignment between and within the complex of *desires, beliefs, values, motivations* and *behaviors*.
- † We are not conflicted with double-mindedness or dissonance in the "new self" spiritual heart.

> I will give thanks to the Lord with my **whole heart**;
> I will recount all of your wonderful deeds. (Ps 9:1 ESV)
>
> Save, O Lord, for the godly one is gone;
> for the faithful have vanished from among the children of man.
> ² Everyone utters lies to his neighbor;
> with flattering lips and a **double heart** they speak.
> (Ps 12:1–2 ESV)

> ¹⁴ But if you have bitter jealousy and selfish ambition in your **hearts**, do not boast and be false to the truth. (Jas 3:14 ESV)
>
> ⁸ Draw near to God, and he will draw near to you. Cleanse your hands, you sinners, and purify your **hearts**, you **double-minded**. (Jas 4:8 ESV)

Clearly, God's interest in renewal, restoration and transformation of the spiritual hearts of humans is infinitely paramount. The status of wholeness and integrity of the spiritual heart indicates how much of the "old self" has been "put off" and how much of the "new self" has been "put on."

At best, the transformation process will resemble the jagged trajectory of an upward trending stock market graphic. It is messy because we are imperfect and we live in an imperfect world. Set expectations accordingly. If we expect perfection, we will be disappointed and our efforts will be perpetually episodic and sporadic. We will be double-minded and waiver between the "old self" belief/behavior systems and the "new self" belief/behavior systems—never internalizing the new so as to replace the old. Our imperfection is a reminder of our need to depend upon Jesus, keep the eyes of our spiritual hearts on Him, and make the glorification of Christ to be our goal so that we have redemptive impact upon those around us.

Two Illustrations in Contrast: Saul and David

I close this chapter with an illustration from the Old Testament of an example of contrast between the spiritual heart of a man who began well, but ended poorly and another who was characterized as a "man after God's own heart" in spite of his tragic failure. The two men are Saul and David.

The story of Saul is probably familiar to most. Samuel anoints Saul as king as recorded in 1 Samuel 10. He looks like king material. God gave *"him another heart"* and the *"Spirit of God ... rushed upon him"* and he prophesied (1 Sm 10:9–13). When Saul first becomes aware of God's selection of him to be king, Saul's *behaviors* manifest a *belief system* relative to where he placed his trust. Initially, he followed Samuel's instructions precisely (1 Sm 10:1–8). However, soon thereafter, we see some hints that all is not well in Saul's spiritual heart. Saul hid among the baggage (1 Sm 10:22)—*behavior* indicative of an anthropocentric orientation and a lack of spiritual self-esteem. His identity was rooted in a *belief system* that associated self-worth and validation with how other fallen humans viewed him. Spiritual leaders within the family of faith emerge from those whose *belief system* reflects trust and confidence in God's purpose and perspective. Security in one's identity accompanies the latter; insecurity accompanies the former.

Later, Saul's lack of an internalized core of truth and principles in his spiritual heart becomes manifest. His anthropocentric focus pivoted upon how he was viewed by those he led. He sought validation from others (e.g. 1 Sm 13). He claimed credit for his son Jonathan's victory (1 Sm 13:4). What he saw with his physical eyes became more real to him than God, truth, and principle. He would not wait upon Samuel (1 Sm 13:8ff). Later, Saul issues commands which are related to his own perceived need for power and control, yet which set up his people for failure (1 Sm 14:24ff).

He disobeys God's specific instructions because "he feared the people" not God (1 Sm 15:24). The remainder of Saul's life is a tragedy of magnanimous proportions. He lived in constant fear and insecurity. He sought to kill David *motivated* by jealousy. The lost potential of Saul's life provides us with a blockbuster example of what happens with each of us on perhaps a lesser stage for that portion of our lives characterized by the "old self."

David's life stands in contrast. When Paul was in Antioch of Pisidia on his first missionary journey and he was recounting the history of God's dealing with Israel, he quotes from 1 Samuel 13:14 indicating that God found in him "*a man after my heart, who will do all my will*" (Acts 13:22 cf. 1 Sm 13:14). As Samuel surveyed the sons of Jesse and he looked upon Eliab, Samuel thought that certainly Eliab was the one God had chosen. But, in contrast to Saul, David was presented last. God says to Samuel—"…*For the Lord sees not as a man sees: man looks on the outward appearance, but the Lord looks on the heart*" (1 Sm 15:7 ESV) Later, the sensitivity of David's spiritual heart to God is disclosed when he realizes that he had taken a census against God's will for a king of Israel. Scripture records that David's spiritual heart was "*struck*" within him (2 Sm 24:10). After David's death and in spite of David's notable failures of adultery and murder and his failures as a father, God's instruction to Solomon contains an incredible statement regarding David—"…*if you will walk before me, as David your father walked, with integrity of heart and uprightness, doing according to all that I have commanded you...*" (1 Kgs 9:4 ESV)

What does the illustration of David tell us? The trajectory or orientation of David's spiritual heart was aligned to God's heart, God's desire for Israel's king and the nation. His *beliefs* regarding the nation were aligned with God's purpose for the nation to be a redemptive agent. He feared or respected the Lord's righteousness. Even though David had notable failures, God's summary statement in 1 Kings 9:4 can be viewed as a holistic assessment of the prevailing trajectory of David's spiritual heart.

The messiness of David's journey of the spiritual heart provides a good illustration of the journey most of us experience. What does the trajectory of your spiritual heart journey of conformity to the image of Jesus look like? Are you adrift on a sea of notions or are you navigating toward the shore of clarity? Are you being filled with the character of Christ as the "new self" resurrects and the "old self" is progressively being put to death experientially? Hopefully, this book provides a biblical framework for navigating through the sea of notions toward a shore with greater clarity in your life as it has in mine and others.

Questions for Consideration:

† How would you assess your heart alignment with God's heart right now?

† If there is any misalignment you can identify, how might you use the process described in this chapter and based upon Romans 6 to address it?

† Have you developed an "old self" complex of beliefs, values, and relational strategies that allows you to be successful in your world, yet you know that it does not reflect the image of Jesus to the world? Do you have inner joy? Do you have contentment?

Glossary of Terms

Habituation – the result of repeating an inter-related set of behaviors, motivations, and beliefs to the point of non-conscious response to relevant stimuli.

Heart – embraces both the material and immaterial nature of a human. It is the repository of the *beliefs* and *values* which inform one's *motivations* (*expectations, emotions*), and observable *behaviors*. It represents the combined function of soul (eternal nature) and body (temporal nature).

Imago Dei – Latin for the image of God. The first humans, Adam and Eve, were created as the image of God. In spite of the fall in the Garden, all humans since have retained a vestige of the imago dei.

Internalize – to make something one's own. There is a world of difference between biblical truth that one academically understands and views as external to himself or herself versus biblical truth that has been fused with the spiritual heart. To the extent that the beliefs, values, motivations, and behaviors of a person are brought into alignment with truth is the extent to which one's identity will be associated with Jesus Christ.

Identity – how we define ourselves. Is our existence defined in terms of what we do, what we accomplish, the country in which we were born and raised, our past, etc. or is our identity defined in terms of how God sees us and our purpose in life as He has defined it in Christ? The former is anthropocentric and the latter, Christocentric.

Spiritual Self Esteem – a phrase referencing how a Christian should value themselves based upon their identity in Jesus Christ in contrast to worldly and anthropocentric measures of value.

Bibliography

Books

Chafer, Lewis S. *Chafer Systematic Theology*. Vol. 6, *Pneumatology*. Dallas, Texas: Dallas Seminary Press, 1948 renewed 1975.

Dickerson, John S. *The Great Evangelical Recession*. Grand Rapids, Michigan: Baker Books, 2013.

ESV Bible. Wheaton, Illinois: Crossway, 2008.

Fair, Steve. *Journey Into the Divided Heart: Facing the Defense Mechanisms That Hinder True Emotional Healing*. Oviedo, Florida: Higher Life Publishing, 2020.

Holmes, Michael W. *The Greek New Testament: SBL Edition*. Lexham Press; Society of Biblical Literature, 2011–2013.

Koch, Kathy, PhD. *Five to Thrive: How to Determine if Your Core Needs are Being Met (And What to do When They're Not)*. Chicago: Moody Publishers, 2005, 2020.

Louw, Johannes P. and Eugene Albert Nida. *Greek-English Lexicon of the New Testament: Based on Semantic Domains*. New York: United Bible Societies, 1996.

The Lexham Hebrew Bible. Bellingham, Washington: Lexham Press, 2012.

Wallace, Daniel B. *Greek Grammar Beyond the Basics*. Grand Rapids, Michigan: Zondervan Publishing, 1996.

Yount, William R. *Created to Learn: A Christian Teacher's Introduction to Educational Psychology*. Nashville, Tennessee: B&H Publishing, 2010.

Websites

Big Daddy Weave. Lyrics to "Redeemed." ZionLyrics at https://zionlyrics.com/big-daddy-weave-redeemed-lyrics (accessed August 17, 2020).

Cherry, Kendra. "20 Common Defense Mechanisms Used for Anxiety," *VeryWellMind* (January 22, 2020), accessed May 2, 2020. https://www.verywellmind.com/defense-mechanisms-2795960

Grohol, John M., Psy.D. "15 Common Defense Mechanisms," *PsychCentral* (June 3, 2019), accessed April 21, 2020. https://psychcentral.com/lib/15-common-defense-mechanisms/

Heron, Melonie, Ph.D. Division of Vital Statistics. "Deaths: Leading Causes for 2017." *National Vital Statistics Reports* 68, no. 6 (June 24, 2019). https://www.cdc.gov/nchs/data/nvsr/nvsr68/nvsr68_06-508.pdf

Jefferson Starship. 1975. *Red Octopus*, "Miracles." LyricsFreak https://www.lyricsfreak.com/j/jefferson+starship/miracles_20070383.html accessed August 18, 2020.

McLeod, Saul. "Defense Mechanisms," *Simply Psychology* (2019), accessed May 2, 2020. https://www.simplypsychology.org/defense-mechanisms.html

McLeod, Saul. "Maslow's Hierachy of Needs," *SimplyPsychology* (March 20, 2020), accessed April 21, 2020. https://www.simplypsychology.org/maslow.html

U.S. Bureau of Economic Analysis, Shares of gross domestic product: Personal consumption expenditures [DPCERE1Q156NBEA], retrieved from FRED, Federal Reserve Bank of St. Louis; https://fred.stlouisfed.org/series/DPCERE1Q156NBEA, June 9, 2020.

About The Author

Steven is married and enjoys jogging and biking on the roads and trails in North Dallas—accompanied by his two dogs whenever possible. Any vacation location that includes the outdoors and hiking with beautiful scenery is God's gift this side of heaven. He also enjoys golf as long as no one is watching.

For more than the past two decades, Steven has led a home-based Bible church and teaching ministry, *The Church of the Servant King*, while completing a Master of Arts in Biblical Studies at DTS in 2001. Steven's forty-year professional career included military service in the United States Marine Corps as an artillery officer, aerial observer, and parachutist followed by staff to leadership roles in financial, accounting (CPA), and information systems' services. Steven retired in 2019 in order to pursue a doctorate of educational ministries degree at Dallas Theological Seminary.

www.ingramcontent.com/pod-product-compliance
Lightning Source LLC
Chambersburg PA
CBHW060524090426
42735CB00011B/2354